GOD, ME, AND SWEET ICED TEA

EXPERIENCING GOD IN THE MIDST OF EVERYDAY MOMENTS

A Devotional Journey

ROSE CHⱭ

D1403290

What people are saying about God, Me, and Sweet Iced Tea …

Short in length. Easy to read. Full of blessings! Rose Chandler Johnson's devotionals make drawing closer to God … doable.

~ Eva Marie Everson, award-winning author of
The Cedar Key Series, Baker/Revell 2011-2013

With faith born of varied life experiences and biblical insights, Rose writes on every person's level. From serving others to keeping a clear conscience, you'll be uplifted, challenged, and inspired. The journal considerations and prayer focus at the end of each chapter offer unique ways to apply these solid truths to your life.

~ Jeanette Levellie, inspirational speaker and author of
Two Scoops of Grace with Chuckles on Top

What I like so much about this devotional book is its wonderful mix of spiritual insights and practical applications. Rose Chandler Johnson is truly adept at finding God in the ordinary and eternal lessons in the everyday moments of life.

~ Ann Tatlock, award-winning author

Rose taps our conscience and heart with her thoughtful, provoking messages. Above the feel-good boost, she asks us to do more; her teacher-self leads us to dig deeper, pray purposefully, and walk deliberately in response.

~ Lisa Lickel, author of *The Last Bequest* and
devotions for *The Word in Season*

Rose Chandler Johnson writes from her heart about universal themes and parallels each devotional with scriptures, which are the eternal threads woven in each story. Not only are her devotionals a delight to read, but you will find them an encouragement in your walk with the Lord, as you apply the golden nuggets of God's Word to your own daily life. This book will encourage you in journaling, prayer, and Scripture reading. I have had the privilege to meet Rose, and I have seen the same grace and love for her Lord expressed in her writing. The devotionals are exceptional in substance and truly touch the heart. This book is a gracefully written tribute to the Lord.

~ Kathleen Ruckman, author,
www.kathleenruckman.com

Through honesty and compassion, Rose lets us see into her life and heart so that we can also examine our own heart. As I read these devotions I was sometimes comforted and other times challenged, but always I thought about the person God sees when He sees me. This devotional is simple enough for the newest believer—or even someone not sure about God—but deep enough to make a life-long Christian feel challenged to go higher. This is a wonderful book and I am thrilled to encourage others to read it and share a copy with friends.

~ Tiffany Colter, author, writer, speaker, writing coach,
and mom, http:www.writingCareerCoach.com

Rose Johnson's devotional offers the reader sweet balm and encouragement through wise and thoughtful reflections on God's grace and provision in the midst of all life can throw at us. Use it as a wonderful way to start the day off right—with God's Word and friendly counsel from a woman whose soul knows.

~ Elizabeth Musser, award winning Christian writer and author
of *The Swan House,* www.elizabethmusser.com

GOD, ME, AND SWEET ICED TEA by ROSE CHANDLER JOHNSON
Published by Lighthouse Publishing of the Carolinas
2333 Barton Oaks Dr., Raleigh, NC, 27614

ISBN 978-1-938499-86-9
Copyright © 2013 by Rose Chandler Johnson
Cover design by: Ted Ruybal: www.wisdomhousebooks.com
Book design by Reality Info Systems Pvt. Ltd., www.realityinfo.com
Author photograph courtesy of Branch Carter

Available in print from your local bookstore, online, or from the
publisher at: www.lighthousepublishingofthecarolinas.com

For more information on this book and the author visit:
http://www.writemomentswithgod.blogspot.com.

Library of Congress Cataloging-in-Publication Data
Johnson, Rose Chandler
God, Me, and Sweet Iced Tea / Rose Chandler Johnson 1st ed.

Printed in the United States of America

For my children
Justin, Jonathan, Anne Marie, Melanie, Katie, and
Robbie,
and their children.
I pray these words will help you experience
the reality of the living Christ every day—forever.

Acknowledgements

First and foremost I'd like to thank my dear friend, Mary Grace Sundy, whose friendship, encouragement, and prayers have been some of my life's greatest treasures. It was she who suggested that I start "writing it all down" regarding my relationship with the Lord. Even more than that, she graciously read devotions I sent to her, long before I ever thought about a published volume. Her questions and commentary—written in her distinctive script—were invaluable to me as I searched deeper into God's Word.

I'd like to express my gratitude to Elizabeth Musser, who said, "Yes, send it to me," when I asked if she might read some of my devotions. She believed in this devotional and encouraged me to keep writing.

My deepest thanks to Patricia Sprinkle whose savvy advice I followed on a route to publication.

Special thanks to Cecil Murphey, whose generosity made it possible for me to attend Write to Publish where I met Eddie

Jones of Lighthouse Publishing of the Carolinas. Thank you, Eddie, for your confidence in me.

Many thanks go to Andrea Merrell, who has been a kind and gracious editor.

And my heartfelt thanks to all my prayer partners and readers. I appreciate you so much. May God richly bless you!

How to Get the Most Out of Your Devotional Journey

∾∾∾

I'm so excited you are reading *God, Me, and Sweet Iced Tea: Experiencing God In the Midst of Everyday Moments.* Whether you've been on this journey for some time, or you're just beginning, this is a journey you don't want to miss. As a believer in the Lord Jesus Christ, you have a personal relationship with the King of kings and Lord of lords. Did you realize that? Just as with any other intimate relationship, you need quality time together in order to grow. This devotional is designed to draw you closer to the heart of God.

Maybe you aren't sure what you believe about God or Jesus Christ. That's okay too. This devotional will give you a good foundation of God's Truth and shine light upon your path.

I can't ever do without God. He is a real and vital part of my day. On a lighter note, sweet iced tea is another thing I can't do without each day. A sweet tea lover since childhood, I remember getting in trouble at the dinner table for drinking all my tea at once, then barely tasting the food on my plate. Still today, I have a glass of iced tea in my hand too much of the time. Both my sister and doctor have tried to wean me off of it, but to no avail.

So, *God, Me, and Sweet Iced Tea* seemed like a light-hearted title for this devotional. For all intents and purposes, your devotional time is a time for intimate conversation, like chatting with a friend as you sip a glass of tea or cup of coffee.

The meditations in this devotional come from my own personal experiences. After filling several spiral notebooks over the years, I drew from those to write these meditations. They reveal insights that result from reflection and journaling about my daily experiences, and meditating on God's Word. I like to focus on God showing Himself in everyday things.

As you sacrifice your time to begin this devotional journey, know that God will honor your desire to learn more of Him. His Word is for your instruction and edification, and you will be strengthened. As you draw close to God, He will draw close to you. As you become more sensitive to His voice, you'll hear Him whisper to your heart.

Questions follow each meditation with spaces for you to write your thoughts. Resist the urge to skip these. Journaling will be well worth the effort. Writing down your thoughts in a relaxed and reflective way will help you gain new understanding as you focus your attention and dig deeper into God's Word.

Customize your devotional time to work for you. Maybe you'll want to read the meditation one day, read the Scripture verses on another day, and write down your thoughts at yet another time. Do whatever works best for you. The important thing is to begin the journey.

I would suggest that you have your favorite Bible in hand when you read, look up the verses in the version you prefer, and think about the Scriptures and what they mean to you. How is the meditation relevant to your life? How does its message apply to you?

As you begin each meditation, expect God to speak to your heart. Begin each devotional time with prayer. I want you to know that I have prayed for you too. I pray that God will use my simple words to speak to your heart and that you will be encouraged and strengthened as you face each new day. I hope you will come to embrace Him as your most trusted friend, always there for you in the midst of every moment. I know He loves me far more than any mortal possibly can. And that is the point of these devotions. I want you to meet my Lord.

Now, let the journey begin …

Contents

The Taste Test

O taste and see that the Lord is good; blessed is the man that trusts in him!

Psalm 34:8 NKJV

Every good cook knows that in order to produce delicious food, you have to *taste* the food as you prepare it. Every fine chef will tell you this is a cardinal rule. And again, when the dish has been served, the taste test is the moment of truth. I love preparing meals for my family to enjoy. Yet I've often had to coax a picky eater to taste a new dish. "You can't say you don't like it if you haven't tasted it," I say.

This Scripture, like an excellent cook, urges you to taste. *O taste and see that the Lord is good ...* Taste—I could coax you, as I've coaxed my children. Taste—I could challenge you. Taste—I will attest to His goodness. *Blessed is the man that trusts in him.* This Scripture is a challenge with a promise. If you give the Lord a try, you will experience His goodness, leading you to trust in Him, resulting in blessings for you. Haven't we all enjoyed the savory delight of a delicious dish well prepared? The goodness of the Lord cannot be compared.

When I made the decision in 1977 to make Jesus the Lord of my life, I tasted. Every day I read a little devotional booklet called *Our Daily Bread*. Its simple format consists of a few verses of Scripture, followed by a prayer. I was faithful to this daily exercise to honor my new commitment to make God a part of my life. I tasted a little each day, not knowing exactly what to expect. Soon, I wanted to know more about God and Jesus Christ. I started reading and praying more. God became more irresistible to me than my daily sweet iced tea, and I grew hungry for His Word, the Bread of Life. It's made all the difference in my life.

I offer you a challenge as you read this devotional: *Taste and see*. I believe that you, too, will attest to the goodness and the blessings of the Lord.

Suggested Reading: Psalm 145:7; Isaiah 63:7; Nahum 1:7

Journaling Considerations: Why do you think chefs always taste the food they prepare?

_____

_____

_____

_____

_____

Have you taken the taste challenge? If you haven't, would you now?

_____

_____

_____

_____

_____

Prayer: _Dear Heavenly Father, nourish our hearts, souls, and minds with your goodness. I praise You for your goodness and your righteousness. In Jesus' name, I pray. Amen._

Today's Sweet Tea Moment: Only Jesus can satisfy the needs of my soul.

Prayer Focus: Those who suffer from brain injuries or disorders which destroy the sense of taste.

Resolutions

And whatever you do, do it heartily,
as to the Lord and not to men.

Colossians 3:23 NKJV

The New Year begins, and with it comes the annual tradition of making resolutions. Many of us set goals which we hope will increase our happiness, prosperity, success, and overall well-being. Most of the goals concern our outward appearance and physical health: weight loss, exercise, and eliminating bad habits. Depending upon the results, which are impacted by many factors, these efforts may produce a temporary improvement in our well-being. However, more lasting results might be achieved if we set goals concerning our spiritual health, which would transform the inner man.

The Scripture verses which could easily sum up a new goal come from Paul's letter to the Colossians: *Whatever you do in word or deed, do all in the name of the Lord Jesus, giving thanks to God the Father through Him* (v. 17). *And whatever you do, do it heartily, as to the Lord and not to men* (v. 23).

Does this apply to everything we say and do? I think it does.

It means that what we say and do should be said and done wholeheartedly, with the Lord's pleasure as the goal, and not man's approval. Focusing our efforts on a resolution such as this would impact every aspect of our lives. Performing every word and deed with Jesus as our focus, offering each word and deed in the name of the Lord Jesus—this is a resolution guaranteed to improve our well-being, and indeed we will grow in fellowship with Him.

Suggested Reading: Colossians 3:16-25

Journaling Considerations: How well do New Year's resolutions work for you?

_____

_____

_____

_____

_____

Read today's verse again. How might you apply that to your life?

_____

_____

_____

_____

_____

Prayer: *Dear Lord God, I am resolved to do everything in word and deed heartily unto you. May I be focused on pleasing you, and may it be my goal to walk closely with you each day. Thank you for the gift of your Son Jesus Christ.*

Today's Sweet Tea Moment: The Lord's pleasure is my goal, and not man's approval.

Prayer Focus: The strength to keep commitments.

What Does the Lord Require?

の〜の

He has shown you, O man, what is good; and what does the LORD require of you;

but to do justly, to love mercy, and to walk humbly with your God?

Micah 6:8 NKJV

My angry teenager yelled at me. "You would be happy if I stayed in my room and had no friends at all!"

That was far from what I wanted *from* her or *for* her. Her words reminded me of the words the children of Israel said to Micah. They wanted to know if the Lord would be pleased with sacrifices of thousands of rams, rivers of oil, and their firstborn children. Of course, that was not what God wanted. Micah stated that God had shown them what was good.

God brought the children of Israel out of slavery in Egypt, parting the Red Sea for their safe passage, and took care of them in the barren desert. You would think they would have always remembered His gracious acts of mercy. Such was not the case. God called for the mountains to be His witnesses against the people of Israel, and asked the people to testify to explain their disobedience to Him. Had they forgotten all He had done for them?

We might ask ourselves the same question. God doesn't want extravagant sacrifices. He wants obedience. He wants us to *do justly* (do the right thing), to *love mercy* (be kind), and to *walk humbly* with Him (aware that He is God).

God does not ask for impossible sacrifices. Obedience is doable.

Suggested Reading: Deuteronomy 10:12-13; Isaiah 1:10-18; Micah 6:1-8

Journaling Considerations: What can I do today to live out this Scripture?

_____

_____

_____

_____

_____

Write about something wonderful the Lord has done for you. Have you told others about it?

_____

_____

_____

_____

_____

Prayer: *Lord God, thank you for your faithfulness and your love and mercy toward me. I will testify of your wonderful works and the mountains will not need to. Help me to do all you require of me. Amen.*

Today's Sweet Tea Moment: God doesn't ask for impossible sacrifices.

Prayer Focus: Pastors and priests who deliver God's Word to the people.

Stop Complaining

*And when the people complained, it displeased
the LORD:*

and the LORD heard it; and his anger was kindled.

Numbers 11:1a KJV

I had gotten into the habit of grumbling and complaining so much that I was disgusted with myself. It was so bad that I wrote "No Whine in 09" across the top of the calendar. And if *I* was tired of hearing myself, then family and friends were surely tired of my litany as well. Only after some serious effort to break the habit did it occur to me that the *Lord* was tired of my complaining too.

The children of Israel complained in the wilderness. On numerous occasions they murmured against Moses and Aaron, *and* the Lord, bemoaning their plight during this pilgrimage. God was vehemently displeased and his anger was kindled against them. Except for the cries and intercession of his servant Moses, God might have consumed that congregation in a moment (Numbers16:41). Ultimately, because of their words, those Israelites died in the wilderness, barred from crossing over into the Promised Land.

Paul uses examples from Israel's wilderness experience to caution against grumbling.

And do not grumble, as some of them did and were killed by the destroying angel (1 Corinthians 10:10 NIV). Paul warns us again to *do everything without complaining or arguing* (Philippians 2:14a NIV). James tells us to be patient in our suffering and says: *Don't grumble against each other, brothers, or you will be judged. The Judge is standing at the door* (James 5:9 NIV).

Jesus spoke these words: *But I say to you that for every idle word men may speak, they will give account of it in the day of judgment. For by your words you will be justified, and by your words you will be condemned* (Matthew 12:36-37 NKJV).

Now I understand that my grumbling and complaining is a lack of faith and a reproach to God at best, and possibly blasphemy, at worst. *I consider that our present sufferings are not worth comparing with the glory that will be revealed in us* (Romans 8:18 NIV).

Suggested Reading: Numbers 11:1; Numbers 14:26-28; Mt.12:36-37; Romans 8:18; 1 Cor. 10:10-11; Philippians 2:14

Journaling Considerations: Do you think counting blessings combats the urge to complain?

_____

_____

_____

_____

_____

Write a list of all the things you are thankful for: loved ones, friends, health, etc.

_____

_____

_____

_____

_____

Prayer: _Dear Father God, Holy One of Israel, have mercy on me. Forgive my idle murmurings against my lot in life. May all that comes into my life be filtered through Your Sovereign Hands._

Today's Sweet Tea Moment: Counting blessings combats the urge to complain.

Prayer Focus: An atmosphere of gratefulness, praise, and love in our homes.

Kindness

The King will reply, 'Truly I tell you, whatever you did
for one of the least

of these brothers and sisters of mine, you did for me."

Matthew 25:40 NIV

When my son Justin was in Iraq in 2003 with the 82nd
Airborne, several news correspondents were embedded with the
troops. Peter Sleeth, with the *Oregonian*, was one such reporter
who posted his stories on the web. I searched for news daily. It
had been several weeks since the war had begun, and we had
not heard a word from Justin. As the weeks passed, fewer stories
regarding the 82nd appeared. Then one day my search yielded
the following link: *Just back from Iraq, see Peter Sleeth's new photo
gallery*. With one click, four pictures of Justin popped onto the
screen.

There was my son, dressed head to toe in full army gear, the
helmet buckled under his chin, his face and hands smeared with
dirt. With a pensive look, he sat crouched on dusty cement steps
facing a little dark haired girl and boy. They, too, were dirty and

13

somber, and sat at his knees looking up into his face. His arms were outstretched to them, as he gave the little girl and barefoot boy sips of water from his bottle. The little boy held a bag of Skittles, which had been in Justin's MRE (meal ready to eat). The caption beneath the picture said Justin was caring for the little children while paramedics cared for their mother nearby. On the following Sunday, which was Easter, the story behind the picture of my son and the little children was a featured story.

When I saw the pictures, my heart overflowed with joy and gratitude to God for his loving kindness to me. I was so eager to have any news of my son. What a miracle to get this glimpse of his activities in Iraq. Out of thousands of soldiers, my son was photographed at that particular moment. Of all the things he could have been doing, his kind deed was captured on camera for me to see.

I can never repay God for that kindness. Justin's deeds were acts of kindness as well. Kindness is a gentle gift from the heart of the giver that does good to the heart of the receiver. Such is the nature of kindness. The giver expects nothing in return.

Paul says in Ephesians 4:32 NKJV: *And be kind to one another, tenderhearted, forgiving one another, even as God in Christ forgave you.* Jesus takes every act of kindness personally. Every act of kindness touches the very heart of God.

Suggested Reading: Proverbs 25:11; Proverbs 31:26; Ephesians 4:32.

Journaling Considerations: Has something happened in your life that you think was a special act of God's kindness?

_____

_____

_____

_____

_____

Have you shown His kindness to someone lately?

_____

_____

_____

_____

Prayer: *Dear Father God, thank you for your tender mercies. You are most gracious and full of loving kindness. Help me to be kind in my words and deeds.*

Today's Sweet Tea Moment: It doesn't cost a cent to give the priceless gift of kindness.

Prayer Focus: Children in need.

What Do Our Hearts Tell?

∽◦∽

I will give you a new heart and put a new spirit
within you;

I will take the heart of stone out of your flesh and give
you a heart of flesh.

Ezekiel 36:26 NKJV

My students are captivated by Edgar Allen Poe's suspenseful tale, *The Tell-Tale Heart*. The narrator relates the story of his vicious deeds in an attempt to prove his sanity. It soon becomes obvious he is insane. He explains how he made up his mind to kill a man, and how he went about doing it. Outwardly, he doesn't give any clues to the thoughts and intents of his heart. In the end, the maddening beating of his own heart drives him to reveal all. I like the moment when my students understand the significance of the story's title. Indeed, Poe was onto something about the heart.

The heart is deceitful above all things, and desperately wicked: who can know it? (Jeremiah 17:9 KJV)

It's a part of our lexicon to label people with such terms

as sweetheart, broken-hearted, hard-hearted, tender-hearted, because the heart is the seat of all emotions. Physically, the heart is the central organ in the body. Spiritually, the heart also takes preeminence. God knows our heart, and it is the Spirit of God that regenerates it, giving us the ability to know Him. We are told to *love the LORD your God with all your heart, with all your soul, and with all your strength* (Deuteronomy 6:5 NKJV). Only the power of God renewing our hearts daily can enable us to do that.

Suggested Reading: Proverbs 4:23; Jeremiah 17:9-10; Jeremiah 31:33; Romans 10:10; 1 John 3:20-21

Journaling Considerations: Examine your own heart in the light of the suggested Scriptures.

What have you discovered? If you've found anything not pleasing to yourself or God, ask Him to take it away and purify your heart.

_____

_____

_____

_____

_____

Prayer: *Dear Heavenly Father, thank you for renewing my heart. May You reign there eternally. Help me to love you with my whole heart.*

Today's Sweet Tea Moment: I will keep my heart clean and pure before God.

Prayer Focus: Those suffering from heart disease.

He Gives Sleep to His Beloved

∞⦾∞

When you lie down, you will not be afraid;

when you lie down, your sleep will be sweet.

Proverbs 3:24 NIV

Friends often comment about the quality of their sleep or their inability to sleep. I am grateful to God that I sleep well, but I remember a time when I didn't. When I was nineteen years old, I got married and within the week, moved 3000 miles away from home. I knew no one in this new place. In addition, my husband's job took him away from home regularly for two to six weeks at a time. Loneliness caused the fears at night to loom large. Every little bump and creak brought imagined horrors which stole my sleep.

One day as I read the Bible, I came across Psalm 4:8: *I will lie down and sleep in peace, for you alone, O Lord, make me dwell in safety.*

This verse became a companion and a promise of God's abiding care. I reasoned with myself in my nighttime prayers. *While I sleep, God is awake, so why not allow myself to rest in*

His everlasting arms and let Him take care of my world? My fears would subside. Sleep was sweet. Today, Psalm 4:8 is literally written on my bedroom wall.

My heart goes out to the many people who experience insomnia due to fears, anxiety, and health conditions. I believe sleep is a blessing God wants to give us. I hope these Scriptures minister peace to you as they did for me and offer you some sweet sleep.

Suggested Reading: Psalm 4:8; Psalm 127:2; Proverbs 3:24

Journaling Considerations: Can you imagine Jesus tossing and turning, worrying over the burdens He carried for souls, or worrying about the trials and tribulations that lay before Him?

_____

_____

_____

_____

_____

How do you think Jesus could sleep during a great storm?

_____

_____

_____

_____

_____

Prayer: *Thank you, Lord, for your blessed sleep. Thank you for taking care of me and my world while I rest in You.*

Today's Sweet Tea Moment: God neither slumbers nor sleeps and He watches over me.

Prayer Focus: Those who are unable to sleep due to fears, anxiety, and health conditions.

For What Is Your Life?

This is the day the LORD has made;
We will rejoice and be glad in it.

Psalm 118:24 NKJV

Nothing throws me off kilter and aggravates my mood like *my* plans being disrupted for the day. I enjoy making a list every morning, and checking off each task on the agenda to keep me focused and efficient. I sure couldn't have foreseen the snow storm for my sunny Georgia town. But as it happened, I had a furlough day, so no problem. I was able to go to the grocery store ahead of schedule. I carried in the groceries as the first flakes began to fall. With a satisfied smile, I thought about *my* plans— bake a fancy cake, make a gourmet meal, read, write, watch a movie—all the makings for a quiet, self-indulgent weekend at home.

Early Saturday morning the phone rang. My daughter told me her home had been without power for twelve hours, and she and my three grandchildren were cold. Of course, they could come over until the power came back on—although *that* was not on my list. I made breakfast for us all—which was not on my list either. Nonetheless, my granddaughter appreciated my grits like they had not been appreciated in some time. We watched *Charlotte's Web*, my old favorite, to the delight of my grandson who was seeing it for the first time. I made lunch, then picked up the sticky macaroni noodles from the table and floor. At naptime, I rocked my grandbaby to sleep, and held her longer than was necessary to get the job done. When they went home after spending all day, the kitchen looked like a storm had gone through it, and none of the items had been checked off my list. But I felt pleased with the day just the same.

My God has a sense of humor.

God was not surprised by the snow storm, nor did He care that not one thing had gotten done according to my plans. God had made this day. "Thy will be done," I pray.

Each day is a pure gift of love from God. I can't make a day. It's not my day to do with as I please, no matter how smugly I plan it out. This experience reminded me that I need to ask Him every morning what is on His list for me. What would He have me do with the day He has given me? For what is my life? It is a vapor that appears for a little time, and then vanishes away.

This is His day. I will rejoice and be glad.

Suggested Reading: Psalm 90:14; Psalm 118:24; James 4:13-15

Journaling Considerations: Are you a list maker? Would you ask God to help you make your list today?

_____

_____

_____

_____

_____

When has God changed your plans for the day in a delightful way?

_____

_____

_____

_____

_____

Prayer: _Dear Heavenly Father God, I thank you for each day of life that you give me. Help me to live it serving you and honoring you. May your will be done in my life._

Today's Sweet Tea Moment: Each day is a gift from God. I will live it for His glory.

Prayer Focus: Redeeming the time for His glory.

Action Speaks Louder than Words

‿⟳‿

*Why do you call me, "Lord, Lord," and do not do what
I say?*

Luke 6:46 NIV

Our actions communicate. Even in subtle ways, our body
language reveals our unspoken feelings. When actions and
words don't jibe, we pick up on that incongruence. The bottom
line is that actions trump words. Leave it to American writer
and humorist Mark Twain to quip: "Action speaks louder than
words, but not nearly as often." Not only does this adage hold
true on a practical level, but also on a spiritual level.

Jesus said, *Not everyone who says to Me, 'Lord, Lord,' shall
enter the kingdom of heaven, but he who does the will of My
Father in heaven* (Matthew 7:21 NKJV). These words of our
Lord cause me to pause and reflect. Lip service does not impress
God. Our actions reveal our love for Him. Jesus said, *If you love
Me, keep My commandments* (John 14:15 NKJV). He takes it
personally when we show kindness and love to our neighbor.
He wants us to feed the hungry, clothe the poor, and take care

of the sick and destitute (see James 2:15-16).

Three times, Jesus asked Simon Peter how much he loved Him. When Simon Peter answered Him each time, Jesus responded with an imperative: *Feed my sheep* (John 21:16 KJV). Jesus expects love to result in action.

John said, *Dear children, let us not love with words or tongue but with actions and in truth* (1 John 3:18 NIV). Let's not be guilty, as Mark Twain pointed out, of speaking so much more than doing.

Suggested Reading: Deuteronomy 10:12; Matthew 7:21; Matthew 25:35-36; John 14:21; John 21:16; 1 John 3:18

Journaling Considerations: In what ways are you demonstrating your love for God?

_____

_____

_____

_____

_____

When was the last time you shared the good news of Jesus Christ?

_____

_____

_____

_____

_____

Prayer: _Dear Father God, thank you for calling me your child, and pouring out your love on me. May I honor You and serve You always, showing by my actions the love I have for You._

Today's Sweet Tea Moment: What have I done for my Lord today?

Prayer Focus: The homeless and forgotten ones.

Obedience Is Better than Sacrifice

*Has the LORD as great delight in burnt offerings and
sacrifices, as in obeying*

*the voice of the LORD? Behold, to obey is better
than sacrifice,*

and to heed than the fat of rams.

1 Samuel 15:22 NKJV

I am the mother of six children. When one of my children listens to me and obeys my directives, I am pleased. Simple obedience brings peace and contentment, whereas disobedience can bring much disappointment, confusion, and grief.

How many times as a parent have I lamented, "If only he had listened to me ... if only she had listened." So much heartache, so many troubles could have been avoided, if only they had listened and obeyed my voice.

Our mature perspective shaped by life experiences allows us as parents to foresee the outcome of some actions and decisions, giving us the wisdom to direct our children to make right choices. When they don't obey and the consequences follow, we endeavor to intervene to keep heartache from turning into heartbreak, setback into disaster, disaster into ruin. We waste countless hours. We lose peace. Simple obedience would have been better than all our efforts to make up for the disobedience.

How much more so can God see all things? How much more does God desire for his children to obey His voice? God demands obedience. He expects us to hearken to His words. Indeed, He says that if we love Him, we will obey His commands (see John 14:21).

Behold, to obey is better than sacrifice, and to heed than the fat of rams (1 Samuel 15:22 NKJV).

Suggested Reading: 1 Samuel 15:10-31

Journaling Considerations: Can you think of a time you had an experience of disobedience as a child? As a parent?

_____

_____

_____

_____

_____

Did the resulting consequences cause you to wish you had listened to the wise counsel of others or God's Word?

_____

_____

_____

_____

_____

Can that incident serve as a reminder to obey God's Word?

_____

Prayer: *Oh God, forgive me for the times I have caused you pain by my disobedience. Thank you for your mercy when I have failed to hearken to your voice. Help me to know your Word, listen to your voice, and be obedient to you at all times.*

Today's Sweet Tea Moment: Am I like King Saul, obeying only in part?

Prayer Focus: Renewed desire to obey God in all things at all times.

Be Still and Know

❦

Be still, and know that I am God: I will be exalted among the heathen,

I will be exalted in the earth.

Psalm 46:10 KJV

Somewhere along the way, I forgot how to be still. In fact, I became the queen bee of busyness. Having six children and then entering the work force, I stayed active from morning until night, sometimes not sitting down all day. I even multitasked in the shower.

I know I'm not alone. In our society, we are expected to be productive. We pride ourselves on how much we can accomplish in a day. Yet it's easy to carry that too far. Overloaded and overwhelmed, consumed with my work, I ignored God's directives to be still and consider His wondrous works.

One day, a dear Christian friend patiently asked me to slow down, and I heeded her advice. At first I actually needed to set the kitchen timer for thirty minutes and practice sitting still. In the early evenings, I sat on the deck with a glass of iced tea, watching the clouds float by and listening to the birds. During these times, my soul became quiet and still. I communed with God in my heart and mind. Like the sun bursting from behind the clouds, joy burst into my heart. I experienced renewed peace as my body relaxed and my breathing became slower and more gentle. Most of all, I experienced a renewed appreciation for who He is, the Creator of the universe and the lover of my soul. I believe God is truly pleased when I practice this Scripture.

Be still and know Him.

Suggested Reading: Job 37:14; Psalm 4:4; Psalm 23:1-3; Psalm 46:10

Journaling Considerations: No questions for journaling today. Instead, sit comfortably, close your eyes, quiet the thoughts running through your mind, and listen to your own breathing. Breathe deeply. As you listen, you might hear God whispering to your heart.

After your period of rest, write down any particular thoughts or impressions that you feel you should take from this devotion.

_____

_____

_____

_____

_____

_____

_____

_____

Prayer: *Dear Father God, it is your accomplishments that are wondrous. I stand in awe of who You are. Help me to be still, and know that You are God. Be exalted in my life and in the earth.*

Today's Sweet Tea Moment: I will give God the time He deserves each day.

Prayer Focus: Those overloaded with responsibilities and cares.

How Can We Know the Way?

Jesus said to him, "I am the way, the truth, and the life.
No one comes to the Father except through me."

John 14:6 NKJV

One of America's great poets, Robert Frost, wrote the popular poem, *The Road Not Taken*. The last stanza has these often quoted lines: "Two roads diverged in a wood, and I—I took the one less traveled by, and that has made all the difference." To me, this poem symbolizes the inevitable choices we all must make. Some choices are so significant that they change forever the very course of our lives.

The poem speaks of only two roads. In reality, it's not that simple. With such liberties in our great society, a myriad of options is available to us for the choices we must make. We must choose schools, homes, communities, careers, spouses, political candidates, and churches. The fact that we have so many options makes choosing even more difficult and sometimes fills us with angst. Each decision matters and takes us on a different path that leads to unknown outcomes.

In spiritual matters, God's Word gives clear direction about the way we should go. When Thomas asked Jesus, "How can we know the way?" Jesus replied: *I am the Way, the Truth, and the Life. No one comes to the Father except through me.* Paul tells us in his letter to the Ephesians that we have access to the Holy Spirit and to God the Father through faith in Jesus Christ. In other words, Jesus Christ is the door through which we must walk in order to enter into God's Kingdom. Believing that God's Word is true, I choose to follow Jesus.

I have regretted many choices I've made that took me down some long, difficult roads. Uncertainty has characterized many of them, but I can say with assurance that I have never regretted my choice to accept Jesus as the Son of God and make Him the Lord of my life. I can say with joy and certainty that my decision to follow Jesus *has* made all the difference.

Suggested Reading: John 14:5-6; Ephesians 2:18; Hebrews 10:20; 1 John 5:20

Journaling Considerations: Can you remember the exact time when you decided to follow Jesus?

_____

_____

_____

_____

_____

Prayer is "knocking" on Jesus' door. Is there something you need to talk to Him about right now?

_____

_____

_____

_____

_____

Prayer: *Dear God, my Father, thank you for Your Son, Jesus Christ, and the sacrifice that He made for me. Thank you that I have access to you and the Holy Spirit through Jesus Christ my Lord. Help me to walk with Him on all of life's roads.*

Today's Sweet Tea Moment: Jesus promises to open the door for *all* who knock.

Prayer Focus: That we might have wisdom and guidance to make good choices.

Let God Be the Judge

Do not judge, or you too will be judged. For in the same way you judge others, you will be judged, and with the measure you use, it will be measured to you.

Matthew 7:1-2 NIV

I failed to do something my sister thought I should do. "Shame on you," she said.

Her condemnation stung. I knew she didn't understand my decision because she had not experienced what I was going through. She didn't understand the difficult choices I faced, and couldn't read my heart and mind.

I'm sure you have experienced this as well. We are all judged in subtle and not so subtle ways every day by those with whom we live and work. Sometimes we aren't even aware a verdict is in on us, and at other times, it's as if the gavel has fallen and all have risen to hear it. And yet, Jesus himself said, *Man, who made me a judge or a divider over you?* (Luke 12:14 KJV)

There is only one Lawgiver and Judge, the one who is able to save and destroy. But you—who are you to judge your neighbor?

(James 4:12 NIV). Psalm 50:6 says: *God is judge himself.* Before Him on Judgment Day, our Creator will judge us all. Until that time, we must be careful not to set ourselves up as judge over others.

Paul says in Romans 14:13 that we should not judge any more, but *judge this rather, that no man put a stumbling block or an occasion to fall in his brother's way.*

Suggested Reading: Psalm 50:6; Matthew 7:1-2; Luke 12:14; Romans 14:13; James 4:11-12

Journaling Considerations: Write about a time when you have judged someone. Did you know all the details?

_____

_____

_____

_____

_____

What do you think about the idea that *with the measure you use, it will be measured to you?*

_____

_____

_____

_____

_____

Complete the following statement: The most important thing for a Christian to remember is:

_____

_____

_____

_____

_____

Prayer: *Dear Holy Father, righteous and almighty, have mercy on me. Forgive me for my sins. Forgive me for judging others. I bow before your throne of grace, and submit myself to You, the Judge of all.*

Today's Sweet Tea Moment: Our God is all-seeing and all-knowing. Only He can judge His creation.

Prayer Focus: Our Supreme Court judges.

Keys to a Successful Life

*This Book of the Law shall not depart from your
mouth; but you shall meditate in it day and night, that
you may observe to do according to all that is written
in it. For then you will make your way prosperous,
and then you will have good success.*

Joshua 1:8 NKJV

No matter how we define it for ourselves, we all want success.
Google the above title and you'll come up with hundreds of
thousands of search results. Visit the bookstore or library and
you'll find dozens of books promising guidance or boasting of
definitive answers on this theme. As believers, we can turn to
God's timeless best-seller, *The Holy Bible*, which tells us how to
have good success.

In the Book of Proverbs (3:1-4 NIV), I read counsel
concerning right living and personalize it for myself and my
children: *My son, do not forget my teaching, but keep my commands
in your heart, for they will prolong your life many years and bring
you prosperity. Let love and faithfulness never leave you; bind them*

around your neck, write them on the tablet of your heart. Then you will win favor and a good name in the sight of God and man.

I get excited about these promises. I want a long life and peace. To understand and to be understood, to have God's favor as well as man's, no matter what your goals ... these are characteristics of success.

The longer I know God, the more convinced I am that all the answers to life's questions can be found in His Word. Attaining success is not an elusive dream if we make it our goal to follow His wise counsel.

Suggested Reading: Joshua 1:8; 1 Chronicles 22:13; 1 Chronicles 29:12; Proverbs 3:1-4; Hebrews 11:6

Journaling Considerations: List all the books you can think of that promise some kind of success if the reader follows the guidelines.

_____

_____

_____

_____

_____

Look on your bookshelves to see how many books you have on philosophy and self-help which promise improved well-being if you will follow their advice.

_____

_____

_____

_____

_____

Might you find answers sooner turning to God's Word first, before you go to other sources?

_____

_____

_____

_____

_____

Prayer: *Dear Lord God, thank you for the wisdom of the ages available to us in Your Word. Give us willing hearts to know You and to live by Your divine counsel.*

Today's Sweet Tea Moment: God rewards those who seek Him.

Prayer Focus: Willingness to know God's Word and live by it.

Forgiveness

∽༠∾

Then said Jesus, "Father, forgive them; for they know not what they do."

Luke 23:34a KJV

Christ's crucifixion and death involved pain, suffering, and humiliation beyond anything any of us will ever endure. He was without sin, yet he took on the sins of the world in order to become the perfect sacrifice for us. He forgave those who caused him pain and suffering. Even as he hung on the cross, he asked God to forgive them, saying they didn't know what they were doing. They became recipients of His compassion and forgiveness.

If we confess our sins, He is faithful and just to forgive us our sins and to cleanse us from all unrighteousness (1 John 1:9 NKJV). God's forgiveness of our sins is the supreme demonstration of His divine mercy and grace.

We are expected to follow Jesus' example, extending forgiveness to all who sin against us. At the close of the Lord's Prayer, Jesus added: *For if you forgive men when they sin against you, your heavenly Father will also forgive you. But if you do not forgive men their sins, your Father will not forgive your sins* (Matthew 6:14-15 NIV).

Peter wanted to know just how often he should forgive someone who sinned against him. To his way of thinking, seven times seemed to be generous, especially in comparison to the law: *an eye for an eye and a tooth for a tooth* (see Matthew 5:38). Jesus' response, *seventy times seven*, implies that our forgiveness must be unlimited. Is such forgiveness humanly possible?

Personally, I've faced some situations where I've told the Lord with my face awash with tears that He's asking me to do something too hard. Sometimes the wrongs against us or our loved ones seem unforgivable. God understands what we are going through. His Son was crucified. Jesus understands. He forgave even in the midst of His suffering. When I feel it's too difficult for me to bend my emotions to God's will, I acknowledge His command for me to forgive, as well as my desire to honor Him by my obedience. When I offer the mercy of forgiveness out of obedience to Christ, eventually my emotions come under the lordship of Christ, and I come to realize that forgiveness is mine to give as well as to receive, thanks to Christ living in me.

Suggested Reading: Matthew 6:12, 14-15; Matthew 18:21-22; Mark 11:25-26; Luke 17:4; Luke 23:34

Journaling Considerations: Why do you think the Lord asks us to forgive *seventy times seven*? Is that humanly possible?

_____

_____

_____

_____

_____

Has someone's sin against you hurt you to the core?

_____

_____

_____

_____

_____

Even as it is, will you pray today's prayer as a love offering to Jesus?

_____

_____

_____

_____

_____

Prayer: *Dear God, according to Your word, I know that You would have me forgive everything that I hold against anyone. By the power of the Holy Spirit working in me, I ask that you give me the will to forgive those who have sinned against me.*

Today's Sweet Tea Moment: The memories will remain, but forgiveness soothes the pain.

Prayer Focus: Those suffering emotional pain due to a lack of forgiveness.

In the Spirit of Meekness

Brothers, if someone is caught in a sin, you who are
spiritual should restore him gently. But watch yourself,
or you also may be tempted.

Galatians 6:1 NIV

It's amazing how clearly we see the mistakes of others. It's easier to call it like it is when we are looking at our brother than when we are looking at ourselves. Knowing that we, ourselves, can and have been tempted, that we make mistakes and fall short, overtaken in our errors, it is wise to remember the saying "but for the grace of God go I."

With this in mind, who better to restore a brother *caught in a sin* than an objective and meek spiritual person? No one really likes to confront a Christian brother or sister about a fault (sin). For me, it's easier to overlook it, let it slide, and not mention it, than it is to suffer the discomfort, or risk the chance of causing conflict in a relationship. But whose place is it to discuss with a Christian brother or sister, a sin that we have observed—a sin they might choose to minimize or deny?

The Scripture instructs us to *restore* that person.

As a friend or relative, we might be the only spiritual person who realizes someone has a particular fault, commits an error, or has a propensity to sin. It's unlikely that he will confess it to the congregation on Sunday. It's unlikely he will drink so much he staggers in the pew, although you know he often stumbles to bed after a night of heavy drinking. It's unlikely he will rob the offering plate, although you know he cheats on his taxes. It's unlikely he will ogle the pretty ladies at church, although you know he looks at inappropriate websites and magazines. When you know these things, whose responsibility is it to discuss these matters with your Christian friend or relative?

We have to ask ourselves if it is our responsibility to approach people in the spirit of meekness with humility, and speak the Truth in love with gentleness. Who can be offended by God's Truth spoken in such a manner? Gentle guidance can help us stay the course. Isn't this so much better than suffering the consequences of our sins at the hands of the world?

Have mercy and reach out to restore a brother. Pray someone will do the same for you.

Suggested Reading: Leviticus 19:17; Isaiah 5:21; Romans 14:12; Galatians 6:1; Ephesians 4:15; 2 Timothy 2:25, James 5:19-20

Journaling Considerations: Have you ever thought you should talk to a friend about a particular problem they were having? Even without their asking for help?

_____

_____

_____

_____

_____

Would you want someone to come to you if you fell into sin? Or would you want them to ignore it and let you go about your way?

_____

_____

_____

_____

_____

Prayer: *Dear God, thank you for friends and relatives who love me enough to speak the Truth in love to me even when it's unpleasant. Give me the grace and the courage to help them when I know they need it. Have mercy on us.*

Today's Sweet Tea Moment: There is no self-righteousness in a true spirit of meekness.

Prayer Focus: Friends, and the courage to heed Paul's advice.

Repentance

He told them, "This is what is written: The Christ will suffer
and rise from the dead

on the third day, and repentance and forgiveness of sins

will be preached in his name to all nations, beginning at
Jerusalem."

Luke 24:46-47 NIV

Some mistakes time can't erase
The chagrin just subsides.
The millstone hangs heavy
Round the neck;
Regret continually derides.

Stumbling blocks to others
No less so to ourselves.
Indeed overcome
We've denied Him;
Yea thrice! Before the cock crowed.

No looking back! Endure
Until Thy kingdom come,
God has graciously provided;
Confess and be ye cleansed;
Repentance is the only apology.

This poem flowed from my heart during a time of personal trial and heartbreak. Later, I realized my sentiments synthesized many Scriptures. Do we hear about the subject of repentance? Do we understand what it means? Webster's Dictionary says it is "the act of turning from sin and dedicating oneself to the amendment of one's life." Jesus died for the remission of our sins, and so that we might repent.

Therefore I will judge you ... every one according to his ways, says the Lord GOD. Repent, and turn from all your transgressions, so that iniquity will not be your ruin (Ezekiel 18:30 NKJV). Repentance is part of God's merciful plan for our salvation. Repentance and salvation go hand in hand.

Suggested Reading: Ezekiel 18:30; Luke 24:46-48; 2 Peter 3:9

Journaling Considerations: Can you feel my heart's cry in the poem?

_____

_____

_____

_____

_____

Is there something you need to turn away from? Or repent of?

_____

_____

_____

_____

_____

Which of the suggested readings speaks to your heart?

_____

_____

_____

_____

_____

Prayer: *Dear Lord God, thank you for providing all I need for the salvation of my soul. Forgive my sins, O Lord, and cleanse me from all unrighteousness.*

Today's Sweet Tea Moment: We all sin and fall short of God's glory.

Prayer Focus: For sinners to repent.

A Good Conscience

Timothy, my child, I am instructing you…so that by following them you may continue to fight the good fight, with faith and a good conscience. By ignoring their consciences, some people have destroyed their faith like a wrecked ship.

1 Timothy 1:18-19 ISV

An incident once happened with my thirteen-year-old son. For nearly an hour he had been receiving (by all appearances) serious and fascinating text messages from a friend. When I walked into the room, he quickly put the phone down and looked at me quite startled. I perceived a sudden flash of embarrassment or guilt.

"What is your friend texting about that is so interesting?" I asked.

"Ah, nothing," my son replied. "Here, I'm turning it off, you take it," he said. His reaction caused me some concern.

The following day we had a conversation about the consciousness of guilt, and that wonderful internal monitor

God has built into the soul of every human being from creation. Adam and Eve knew they had violated God's instructions. *Then the eyes of both of them were opened, and they knew that they were naked; and they sewed fig leaves together, and made themselves coverings* (Genesis 3:7 NKJV). It's impossible to keep a good conscience while deliberately disobeying God.

With proper training, the conscience can be a true and sensitive inner guide that warns us to resist wrongdoing, making us feel guilty when we don't. We should never override the still small voice of conscience, even though free will shouts to have its way. We are always at liberty to choose to heed our conscience or not. Paul's instructions and warnings to Timothy imply that a willful disregard of conscience can destroy one's faith like a wrecked ship. I believe that conscience, too, can be snuffed out by a soul that persists in sin.

Suggested Reading: Genesis 3:7; 2 Corinthians 1:12; 1 Timothy 1:5-7, 19; Hebrews 9:14; Hebrews 13:18

Journaling Considerations: What is the greatest challenge you have faced as it concerns ignoring your conscience?

_____

_____

_____

_____

_____

Explain what you think Paul means by: *I exercise myself, to have always a conscience void of offence toward God, and toward men* (Acts 24:16).

_____

_____

_____

_____

_____

Prayer: *Dear Lord God, I want to keep a good conscience. Give me the understanding and the will to conduct myself in accordance to your Word. Forgive me of my sins.*

Today's Sweet Tea Moment: The blood of Christ will cleanse my conscience.

Prayer Focus: For parents to train their children well.

Let us Pray

Pray without ceasing.

1 Thessalonians 5:17 KJV

Early one morning, a colleague invited me to chat over a cup of coffee. I told her I'd meet her in a few minutes, because I wanted to pray first.

Looking puzzled, she asked, "Why?"

I gave her some quick answer, but I should have said more.

Prayer is a privilege for those of us who believe. We can call upon the name of the Lord, and while we are speaking, He hears us. Prayer is our way of letting God know we need Him every moment. It's free to all and requires no fancy clothes or special degrees. Anyone can pray.

Paul speaks boldly on prayer. He writes to the Thessalonians to *pray without ceasing.* He writes to the Philippians that *in every thing by prayer and supplication with thanksgiving let your requests be made known unto God.* He instructs the Colossians to *continue in prayer,* and tells Timothy, *I will therefore that men pray everywhere.*

In other words, prayer is more than a ritual to be performed in church or in a special place dedicated to prayer in our home. Prayer can take place anywhere, about anything, at any time. There is nowhere that we, as children of God, can be that God will not hear us.

Jesus prayed. Therefore, let us pray.

Suggested Reading: Genesis 4:26; 1 Chronicles 16:7-36; Isaiah 65:24; Philippians 4:6; 1 Thessalonians 5:17; 1 Timothy 2:8; James 5:16

Journaling Considerations: What do you think of Paul's teachings on prayer? Do you think he really meant it when he said to *pray without ceasing*?

_____

_____

_____

_____

_____

How might your life be changed if you took everything to God in prayer?

_____

_____

_____

_____

_____

Prayer: *Dear Father God, thank You that I can draw close to You in prayer. Thank You for welcoming me into Your presence and hearing me when I call.*

Today's Sweet Tea Moment: God hears me when I call to Him.

Prayer Focus: Praise God for the privilege of communicating with Him through prayer.

Reality of the Indwelling Christ

*Don't you know that you yourselves are God's temple
and that God's Spirit lives in you?*

1 Corinthians 3:16 NIV

From the moment of salvation, the Spirit comes into our hearts. This is what I've been taught and believe. I have believed by faith, and have an intellectual knowledge of the truth of God's Word. I'm grateful that God, by His grace, also gives us real-life experiences which confirm His reality in us. There's nothing quite like the *knowing* that comes from experience. Let me share one such incident with you.

Early one morning, I was in my classroom preparing for the day's activities. My students were quietly working in groups on a warm-up activity, which gave me a few minutes to work at my desk. I gazed across the room where a large bright window caught my eye. Several potted plants thrived there in the light. My thoughts turned to God and I said, "I need some encouragement, Lord. I need a special touch from You today."

No sooner had those words passed through my consciousness

than I heard, *Go touch that leaf.* When the words popped into my head, I knew the Lord was speaking to me. Without hesitation, before I could question myself, I walked directly to the window and grasped a leaf between the palms of my hands. As soon as I touched that leaf, the words continued: *You cannot see it or feel it, yet life is coursing through this plant. That's how I am in you.*

As I stood holding the leaf, nothing marvelous happened on the outside. On the inside, however, I was filled to overflowing with peace, joy, and the blessed assurance of His presence. An awesome awareness unlike any I had ever had before of the omnipresence of God filled me. He was all around me, like the air I breathe, surrounding me and within me, invisible, yet my very life. The awareness of this reality stayed with me for days.

Now, years later, I know that God, by His mercy and kindness, taught me a truth that day. He gave me the special touch I needed. Because of that special moment of grace, I have a heightened sense of my place in Him and of His Spirit within me. I can say as Paul did: *For in Him we live, and move, and have our being* (Acts 17:28a).

Suggested Reading: John 14:19-23; 1 John 4:13-15

Journaling Considerations: Do you have a request for God today? Would you ask God to give you that special touch you need from Him?

_____

_____

_____

_____

_____

Even though you can't see Him, do you trust that God's Spirit lives in you?

_____

_____

_____

_____

_____

Prayer: *Dear Father God, thank You for loving us so much that You sent your Son Jesus Christ to be the Savior of the world. Thank You He is mine, and the Holy Spirit dwells in me. Teach me all that You have for me to learn of You.*

Today's Sweet Tea Moment: It's a divine mystery—we dwell in Him and He dwells in us.

Prayer Focus: Those who feel that God is far away.

The Fruit of the Spirit

∽∘∾

But the fruit of the Spirit is love,
joy, peace, patience, kindness,
goodness, faithfulness, gentleness, and self-control.

Galatians 5:22-23 ISV

Years ago I received a capiz shell wind chime as a gift. Each brightly colored shell was shaped like a fruit. According to my friend, these fruits represented the Fruit of the Holy Spirit. I memorized the verse and hung the wind chimes in front of the kitchen window. With each delicate tinkling, I remembered the list of virtues and wondered how it would be possible for all of these fruits to become evident in my life.

Paul wrote to the churches in Galatia, encouraging them to live by faith in Jesus Christ rather than giving in to their own fleshly desires. What results when people give in to the desires of a sinful nature?

Now the works of the flesh are obvious: sexual immorality, impurity, promiscuity, idolatry, witchcraft, hatred, rivalry, jealousy, outbursts of anger, quarrels, conflicts, factions, envy, murder, drunkenness, wild partying, and things like that. I am telling you now, as I have told you in the past, that people who practice such things will not inherit the kingdom of God (Galatians 5:19-21 ISV). When we live according to our sinful natures, we hurt ourselves and others and, in effect, reject the power available to us through the Holy Spirit.

Paul goes on to say, *But the fruit of the Spirit is love, joy, peace, patience, kindness, goodness, faithfulness, gentleness, and self-control. There is no law against such things. Now those who belong to the Messiah Jesus have crucified their flesh with its passions and desires. If we live by the Spirit, let's also be guided by the Spirit* (Galatians 5: 22-25 ISV).

A life in harmony with the Holy Spirit, and consequently in accordance to God's Word, will produce the Fruit of the Spirit.

Suggested Reading: Galatians 5:16-26

Journaling Considerations: Is the Fruit of the Spirit evident in your life? Which ones?

_____

_____

_____

_____

_____

Are any of the works of the flesh Paul listed evident in your life?

_____

_____

_____

_____

_____

How does this Scripture reading inspire or challenge you?

_____

_____

_____

_____

_____

Prayer: *Dear Father, thank you for the gift of your Holy Spirit. Help me to live in harmony with your Word and the Holy Spirit. Forgive me when I give in to sinful desires. I want my life to produce a beautiful bounty of spiritual fruit. All to Your glory, Christ Jesus. Amen.*

Today's Sweet Tea Moment: Desire the Fruit of the Spirit.

Prayer Focus: Those who struggle to overcome fleshly desires.

A Life of Service

*For whoever wants to save his life will lose it, but
whoever loses his life for me will find it.*

Matthew 16:25 NIV

I remember the time, some twenty or so years ago, when my little children revolved around me like the planets circle the sun. I felt like I was holding them all in place, but God was holding us all. He was ever present.

One especially exhausting day, as I was changing a diaper and hurriedly juggling many tasks, I said aloud in exasperation, "I don't have a life!"

Without hesitation, the Lord responded emphatically to my words. In my spirit, I heard: *No, you don't have a life. Didn't I tell you that whoever will save his life shall lose it, and whoever will lose his life for My sake shall find it?*

These words came directly to me, personal and real—interjected into my train of thought by a voice of authority.

At that moment I knew the Lord had spoken to me. I realized I was doing exactly what He wanted me to do; I was taking care of the needs of my family. My service to them was not an obligation, but a holy calling—a vocation to serve the needs of those in my care.

Jesus became a servant to all, taking on the form of a servant in his earthly life. His service was love in action. His selfless love, for our redemption and God's glory, is a model for all believers. It is with this same spirit that we can dedicate our lives to His service. By doing so, we are strengthened to give of ourselves to others, in our families and beyond, as we go about our everyday lives.

Suggested Reading: Matthew 16:24-26; Matthew 25:31-46; 1 Corinthians 9:19; Philippians 2:7-8

Journaling Considerations: Can you think of times when your service to others causes you frustration? Self-pity?

_____

_____

_____

_____

_____

What encouraging words would you like to hear at those times?

_____

_____

_____

_____

_____

In your own words, describe what Paul means in 1 Corinthians 9:19.

_____

_____

_____

_____

_____

Prayer: *Dear God, I want to be at your service, doing whatever it is that you have called me to do this day. Strengthen me to serve. Give me the love I need to put into my actions. Show me the tasks you have called me to do, that I may live my life for Your glory.*

Today's Sweet Tea Moment: What would Jesus do?

Prayer Focus: Those who devote their lives to God's service by serving others.

Perfect Peace

You will keep him in perfect peace,
whose mind is stayed on You,

because he trusts in You.

Isaiah 26:3 NKJV

I visited the home improvement store recently and enjoyed the background music as I browsed the aisles. The cashier was listening too, because as I checked out, she actually started singing the lyrics of the catchy tune filling the airwaves.

That's when it got stuck in my head. I first noticed it as I waited at the traffic light. I was singing it in my mind. By the time I got to the grocery store, I was singing it out loud. It wasn't even a song I liked. That wasn't the end of it. It happened again the next day, and the next. When I started writing this, it happened again.

Do you know what I mean? Have you ever had a song stuck in your head that wouldn't go away? Maybe you heard it on the radio, in church, or in the grocery store, and it played over and over like a broken record.

Unfortunately, negative thoughts, self-doubts, painful memories, and worry can get stuck in our minds as well. Even though we don't like it, those negative thoughts can play over and over again, causing us to lose our peace.

For our mental and spiritual health, it's important to control our thoughts.

In Philippians 4:8-9 (NIV), Paul gives us a list: *Finally, brothers, whatever is true, whatever is noble, whatever is right, whatever is pure, whatever is lovely, whatever is admirable—if anything is excellent or praiseworthy—think about such things. Whatever you have learned or received or heard from me, or seen in me—put it into practice. And the God of peace will be with you.*

Could he have been any more direct? Here we have God's will in simple terms. Paul said *Think about such things.* I like the promise he gives: *The God of peace will be with you.*

Suggested Reading: Psalm 19:14; Isaiah 26:3; John 14:27; 2 Corinthians 10:3-5; Philippians 4:8-9

Journaling Considerations: Make a list of some negative thoughts that have worried you lately.

_____

_____

_____

_____

_____

List the eight things Paul tells us to think about.

_____

_____

_____

_____

_____

Prayer: *Dear Lord, as the Psalmist said, "May the words of my mouth, and the meditations of my heart, be acceptable in your sight." Help me bring every thought into conformity to your will.*

Today's Sweet Tea Moment: When I am preoccupied with stormy thoughts and worries, I will fix my mind on the One who calms the storm.

Prayer Focus: Those tormented by unholy thoughts.

He Shall Be like a Tree

∽∾∾∾

He shall be like a tree planted by the rivers of water, that brings forth its fruit in its season,

whose leaf also shall not wither; and whatever he does shall prosper.

Psalm 1:3 NKJV

I love trees. Contemplating their serene beauty gives me a sense of peace and contentment. Maybe it's because I grew up living at the edge of dense woods. They were my magical playground.

In elementary school, I memorized the poem, *Trees*, by Joyce Kilmer: "I think that I shall never see a poem as lovely as a tree… Poems are made by fools like me, but only God can make a tree."

I thought this had to be the most amazing poem ever written. Recently, a personal experience made me realize my deep connection to trees.

A huge pine tree flourished about seventeen feet from my kitchen window until I decided to build a brick patio. The stately pine was cut down. The next morning I came downstairs as usual to make coffee. Something was not right. I turned three hundred and sixty degrees a couple of times, trying to figure out what was wrong. That's when I realized the tree was missing. The tree that I'd enjoyed for twenty years was no longer standing its quiet watch over my home. I can't even tell you how much I regretted having it removed. I missed that tree, like an old friend gone forever. For weeks, I second-guessed myself about having it cut down. To make my peace, I prayed and planted a cherry tree near where the faithful pine had stood.

David's words in the first Psalm capture my attention with promises for one who delights in God's laws and disciplines himself to avoid ungodly associations. I say *yes* to being like a tree planted by rivers of water, my leaves never withering… "Looking at God all day, and lifting my arms to pray." (Kilmer)

Suggested Reading: Psalm 1:1-3; Psalm 52:8; Psalm 92:12-14

Journaling Considerations: Read the Scriptures for today. What images and impressions come to mind?

_____

_____

_____

_____

_____

How might you apply those thoughts to your life?

_____

_____

_____

_____

_____

Prayer: _Dear Father God, make my roots grow deep in the soil of your Word and feed my soul with living water so that it never thirsts. I delight in Your law. Help me to meditate on it day and night._

Today's Sweet Tea Moment: We rely on trees for the air we breathe, and vice versa.

Prayer Focus: Conservation and tree-planting efforts.

Depart from Evil

Woe unto them that call evil good, and good evil.

Isaiah 5:20a KJV

No one doubts that evil is a powerful and destructive reality in the world. Scripture instructs us over and over to abhor evil, depart from it, abstain from it, remove our foot from it, and not to follow it, lust after it, or imagine it. That great saint, Job, tormented and tempted by Satan, told us that the fear of the Lord is wisdom, and to depart from evil is understanding. One would think common sense would compel us to depart from evil and actively avoid it. Yet we know this is not always the case.

God's Word clarifies His expectations for us concerning evil. He expects us to know the difference between good and evil. This leads us to ask unavoidable questions regarding right and wrong. Indeed, it is imperative for us to understand what constitutes evil. We associate evil with Satan, and all that is characteristic of him who kills, steals, and destroys lives and human souls. Yet, if evil were so crystal clear, the road to heaven would not be so narrow. All things evil are not flagged with a fiery X that warns of danger and death. We must heed the warning that comes to us on God's authority, and discern what constitutes good and evil. The word in Isaiah is a strong warning to those who get it wrong, believing that evil is good, and good is evil.

From time immemorial, what man calls good or evil is as individual as personalities, opinions, and societal norms. We cannot rely on the world to illuminate questions regarding right and wrong. In fact, many actions which man deems legal and appropriate are indeed evil. We can't judge according to the passing trends of societies, nor trust the nonsense of the mass media to enlighten our hearts and minds. All are subject to the pressures and whims of corruptible man whose heart is *deceitful and desperately wicked* (Jeremiah 17:9).

How can we know the difference between good and evil? We need to seek God's mind on matters, learn what He calls good and evil, and measure all against the incorruptible authority of His Word.

Suggested Reading: Psalm 34:14; Proverbs 4:27; 1 Corinthians 10:6; 1 Peter 3:10-11

Journaling Considerations: What comes to your mind when you consider what society has deemed right that is contrary to Scripture?

_____

_____

_____

_____

_____

Jesus taught us to pray: *Deliver us from evil.* Why do you think He included that in the prayer?

_____

_____

_____

_____

_____

Prayer: *Dear Lord God, teach me Your perspective so that I might rightly discern good and evil. Sharpen my focus to see as You see. Put in me the will to avoid evil, and to seek Your pleasure. Deliver us from evil.*

Today's Sweet Tea Moment: God is good and greatly to be praised.

Prayer Focus: Wisdom and discernment for all who seek the heart of God.

Today Has Enough Troubles
of Its Own

Therefore do not worry about tomorrow,
for tomorrow will worry about itself.

Each day has enough trouble of its own.

Matthew 6:34 NIV

So much has been written about worry, I'm sure I can't say anything new. It's part of the universal human condition. Jesus knew our condition when he gave us this principle for living worry-free. Recently I read several of Dale Carnegie's books. He teaches that we should live in "day-tight compartments" in order to overcome worry. That concept seems to be just another way of saying: *Each day has enough trouble of its own.*

That advice sounds simple, yet it's so difficult to put into consistent practice in our everyday lives. Jesus spoke about this in his Sermon on the Mount: *Do not worry about tomorrow.* Don't worry. Don't even think about it. It's not here yet, and it may never come. *For tomorrow will worry about itself.* Tomorrow we will deal with tomorrow's business. *Each day has enough trouble of its own.* There is enough to worry about just dealing with today.

When each day is over, it becomes that wonderful part of our story called the past. Once lived, it's finished, saved for all eternity.

Trust Jesus to help you live this day as best you can, so you can enjoy the treasure of a life well-lived.

Suggested Reading: Matthew 6:34; Philippians 4:6; 1 Peter 5:7

Journaling Considerations: What do you think the following phrase means? *Each day has enough trouble of its own.*

_____

_____

_____

_____

_____

Do you think God is bigger than all your problems?

_____

_____

_____

_____

_____

Prayer: *Dear Heavenly Father, I want to live each day without worrying about the past or the future. Help me live each day trusting You without worry and care. Thank You for caring for me.*

Today's Sweet Tea Moment: We are warned not to worry—it's wasteful and wrong.

Prayer Focus: That we might know His peace.

Your Adversary the Devil

Be self-controlled and alert. Your enemy the devil prowls around like a roaring lion looking for someone to devour. Resist him, standing firm in the faith, because you know that your brothers throughout the world are undergoing the same kind of sufferings.

1 Peter 5: 8-9 NIV

Satan claims authority over the world. When Jesus was on this earth, Satan endeavored to tempt even Christ. By so doing, he attempted to derail the plan of God and the work that Jesus came to do (see Matthew 4:1). Christ was victorious. By the power of His sinless life, death, and resurrection, He destroyed the works of the devil, and triumphed over sin and death. It's through His power in us that we, as believers, are able to resist. It is our faith in the Lord Jesus Christ that wins the battle against Satan and his work in our lives.

This is, however, an active, ongoing process. For this reason, Peter warns us to *be self-controlled and alert.* As long as we are living in this world, we will have to deal with our adversary the devil, who pulls out all the stops in his attempts to cause us to give up our faith in God. Satan desires to derail God's plan for our lives.

Jesus' words to Simon Peter give us insight into Satan's intentions: *Simon, Simon, Satan has asked to sift you as wheat. But I have prayed for you, Simon, that your faith may not fail. And when you have turned back, strengthen your brothers* (Luke 22:31-32 NIV). Jesus gives us a graphic image of Satan hungering for Simon Peter's soul. Jesus prayed that Simon's faith would not fail.

Faith in the Lord Jesus Christ overcomes Satan. Paul instructed the believers in Ephesus to put on the spiritual armor with which to withstand the spiritual warfare that raged against them: *Above all, taking the shield of faith with which you will be able to quench all the fiery darts of the wicked one* (Ephesians 6:16 NKJV).

Even Job, tormented as he was by Satan, eventually experienced victory over him in his life. *Resist the devil and he will flee from you* (James 4:7 KJV).

Suggested Readings: Luke 22:31; Ephesians 6:11-13; James 4:7; 1 Peter 5:8-10; 1 John 3:8

Journaling Considerations: Jesus prayed that Peter's faith would not fail. Why do you think he prayed that particular prayer?

_____

_____

_____

_____

_____

Would you like Jesus to pray that same prayer for you?

_____

_____

_____

_____

_____

Prayer: *Dear Lord God, I pray that my faith in the Lord Jesus Christ never fails. Keep it strong and unwavering. Help me to walk in victory each day with You as my strength and my shield.*

Today's Sweet Tea Moment: My faith is the victory that overcomes the world.

Prayer Focus: Strengthen our most holy faith.

God Has Not Given Us the Spirit of Fear

The LORD is my light and my salvation;
whom shall I fear?

The LORD is the strength of my life:
of whom shall I be afraid?

Psalm 27:1 KJV

The Apostle John said, *Fear has torment* (see 1 John 4:18). I agree—fear *does* have torment. Perusing a popular magazine, I read a brief story about a man who had taken his own life. His wife said "he lived in fear" of a certain dreaded event coming to pass. That fear tormented him.

I lived for many years at or below the poverty level. Sometimes I would catch myself living in fear of lack—lack of enough money to pay the bills, to provide for my family, to take care of our needs. I would catch myself living in fear of illness—which results in lack.

I am a single parent. Single parents know what it means to fear. Fear *has* torment.

God promises to strengthen us. He promises to help us. *Fear not, for I am with you; be not dismayed, for I am your God. I will strengthen you, yes, I will help you, I will uphold you with My righteous right hand* (Isaiah 41:10 NKJV). Are we convinced this is true?

Paul wrote to Timothy that *God has not given us the spirit of fear; but of power, and of love, and of a sound mind* (2 Timothy 1:7). In reality, God has not given us the *spirit of fear* we sometimes feel—the fear that inhibits us and gnaws at our peace of mind, damaging our physical bodies and stealing our joy. What grace He bestows on us!

Our God loves us with a perfect love. As we receive that love, we can also know He is our helper, and we need not fear. If you have a fearful heart, I say to you as Isaiah did: *Be strong, fear not* (Isaiah 35:4 KJV).

Suggested Reading: Psalm 27:1; Isaiah 35:4; Isaiah 41:10; Matthew 10:28; Hebrews 13:6; 1 John 4:18

Journaling Considerations: Meditate on the following verse from the 23rd Psalm: *Yea though I walk through the valley of the shadow of death, I will fear no evil, for Thou art with me,* and write your thoughts.

_____

_____

_____

_____

_____

What do you think of the verse that says: *Perfect love casts out fear?*

_____

_____

_____

_____

_____

Prayer: *Dear God, You are my light and my salvation. Deliver me from all my fears. Thank you for your perfect love. Let your power be in my life.*

Today's Sweet Tea Moment: God's perfect love will cast out fear.

Prayer Focus: Those who live in fear.

No Man Can Tame the Tongue

～◌～

But the tongue can no man tame;
it is an unruly evil, full of deadly poison.

James 3:8 KJV

Try as I might, I couldn't seem to stop myself from adding comments when a group at work started "discussing" other colleagues—behind their backs, no less. Too often the discussions turned to second-guessing, critiquing, and judging—in other words, gossiping and backbiting. Even when I only listened, my rapt attention indicated tacit approval. This is not professional behavior, nor is it Christian behavior. My conscience convicted me every time.

James 4:11-12 NIV says: *Brothers, do not slander one another. Anyone who speaks against his brother or judges him speaks against the law and judges it. When you judge the law, you are not keeping it, but sitting in judgment on it. There is only one Lawgiver and Judge, the one who is able to save and destroy. But you—who are you to judge your neighbor?* These words seem to have been written just for me.

Keeping my tongue from wagging was definitely harder than any diet I'd tried. James has much to say about this *unruly evil.* He says *the tongue can no man tame.* Man can control all manner of heavy machinery, and all manner of living things, but not that little member of the body! If no man can tame it, who can? Only God.

I started praying every morning on the way to work about keeping my mouth shut, avoiding all gossip and backbiting. It was easy to avoid the ones who started the talk—walk away or walk out when conversations trailed off down that path. I could even say, "I'd rather not discuss that without so-and-so here." Granted, after it became apparent that I disapproved of the behavior, I felt like *I* became the topic of conversation. For a while, I was uneasy. Then I forgot about it. For me, at least, the atmosphere became less stressful and more conducive to accomplishing the tasks at hand. My conscience no longer condemned me.

Suggested Reading: Proverbs 16:28; Proverbs 26:20; James 4:11-12

Journaling Considerations: What do you think of James 3:8? *But the tongue can no man tame; it is an unruly evil, full of deadly poison.*

_____

_____

_____

_____

_____

Have you experienced a tongue's deadly poison?

_____

_____

_____

_____

Prayer: *Dear Father God, my Creator, you are the Judge and Lord of my life. Have mercy on me. I want my tongue under your control. Forgive me for hurting anyone by my words.*

Today's Sweet Tea Moment: The tongue is a fire—a world of iniquity.

Prayer Focus: The judges and court system in our country.

Feet of Clay

‿∘∿

It is better to trust in the LORD than to
put confidence in princes.

Psalm 118:9 KJV

Once upon a time, there was a parent (teacher, preacher, politician ... you fill in the blank with whomever applies in your life) whom I highly esteemed. In my eyes, he was wiser and more virtuous than any other. I thought he could do no wrong. Then, events occurred in which this highly esteemed person behaved in ways inconceivable to me and contrary to the godly image I held of him. As the dust of dismay and disillusionment cleared from my eyes, I saw this person for who he really was—just a mortal man with feet of clay.

Most of those whom we look up to, do not disappoint us. Still, we must be mindful that God alone is worthy of our adoration. He is the creator who molded us from clay.

But now, O LORD, You are our Father; we are the clay, and You our potter; and all we are the work of Your hand (Isaiah 64:8 NKJV). The Psalmist advises us not to put our trust in princes, nor man, in whom there is no help. Our help comes only from the Lord, who made heaven and earth. The Scripture in Jeremiah gives us a beautiful story of the potter, who by his will and design, molds and forms the clay any way he chooses. We are indeed as clay in the potter's hand. We do well to remember that.

Daniel, by the power of God, was enabled to interpret the prophetic dream of King Nebuchadnezzar. Daniel described the great image, representative of earthly kingdoms, as being made of gold, silver, brass, iron, and *feet part of iron and part of clay*. When the image was smote upon the feet, it broke to pieces and the whole thing collapsed and crumbled *like the chaff of the summer thrashing floors*. Christ is victorious, and our sovereign God is above all. We can have heroes, and admire people, but we need to keep in mind that God is our sovereign creator, and we all have feet of clay.

Suggested Reading: Psalm 118:9; Psalm 146:3; Isaiah 64:8; Jeremiah 17:5; Jeremiah 18:1-6; Daniel 2:31-35

Journaling Considerations: Does the situation I described sound like a familiar one to you? Has something like this happened to you? Write about it right now.

_____

_____

_____

_____

_____

Prayer: *O Mighty God, creator of heaven and earth, You formed me and knew me while I was yet in my mother's womb. I thank You and praise You for who You are. I will put no one else above You on the throne of my heart. Have mercy on me, Your creation.*

Today's Sweet Tea Moment: God is the potter; I am the clay.

Prayer Focus: Political leaders, parents, teachers, pastors—all those who have the power to influence a person's life for good or evil.

Besides Change, What Can We Depend On?

⌘

The LORD is my rock; and my fortress,
and my deliverer;

the God of my rock; in him will I trust…

2 Samuel 22:2-3a KJV

Through the years, harmonious and happy living has been my desire for me and my children. With much diligence and a sense of purpose, this working mother of six children maintains a certain balance—most of the time. My home is a peaceful oasis in a chaotic world—most of the time. Life goes smoothly—most of the time. Until the unexpected happens: auto accidents, illnesses, financial upsets, death. Life is interrupted; peace is disrupted.

Changes naturally occur. It might be as simple and immediate as a new supervisor at work, or as life-changing as the death of a loved one. A child grows up and moves away from home. Oh, why can't life flow smoothly and peacefully all the time? Why can't life stay just as we like it, all the time? We long for heaven on earth.

Jesus told us our Heavenly Father *makes his sun to rise on the evil and on the good, and sends rain on the just and on the unjust.* As the saying goes: "In every life some rain must fall." The wise Solomon told us: *To every thing there is a season.* Such is life. Then besides change, what can we depend on?

We can depend on our unchanging Savior, *Jesus, the Messiah … the same yesterday and today—and forever!* We can depend on the God of our salvation, our Rock, and put our trust in the One who *is* for all eternity. He is the Alpha and the Omega, the beginning and the end. God is the only unchanging variable in our lives.

Suggested Reading: Deuteronomy 32:4; 2 Samuel 22:1-4; Ecclesiastes 3:1-8; Matthew 5:45; 1 Corinthians 10:4; Hebrews 13:8; Revelation 1:11

Journaling Considerations: Have you ever lamented the changes in your life?

_____

_____

_____

_____

_____

Can you think of some changes that unsettled you and caused you to look to God?

_____

_____

_____

_____

_____

Prayer: _Dear God, the rock of my salvation, I put my trust in you. Thank you for being eternal God, my fortress. You are the anchor of my soul._

Today's Sweet Tea Moment: Build all on the sure foundation of Christ.

Prayer Focus: That all may come to know Him.

Strangers in a Strange Land

❦

If you call "Father" the one who judges everyone impartially according

to what they have done, you must live in reverent fear

as long as you are strangers in a strange land.

1 Peter 1:17 ISV

I love being a citizen of the United States of America—a nation of immigrants from all over the world—so it was with much enthusiasm that I taught English to speakers of other languages. In addition to language, I also taught our culture and history, and endeavored to impart to my students an appreciation for the American way of life. Assimilation and acculturation are objectives for newcomers in order to help them overcome the feelings of alienation in a foreign land. When immigrants *melt* into the life and culture of America, they begin to feel they belong here.

While reading the above Scripture in 1 Peter, I realized that we, as Christians, must do just the opposite of those students. Rather than assimilate the ways of our world and *melt* into the culture, it is our calling and challenge to live in this world, yet keep ourselves *unspotted from the world* (James 1:27). We *are* strangers in a strange land.

On this journey of faith, we are called to holy living. As we live a sanctified life, we come to realize all this world has to offer is vanity, and that only God can give us the true desires of our hearts. Peter beseeches us as strangers and pilgrims to live in reverential fear of God the Father. We must live according to His Holy Word, not being conformed to the customs and ways of this world.

The Psalmist said: *I am a stranger in the earth: hide not thy commandments from me* (Psalm 119:19 KJV). As we walk with Him in faith on our way to heaven, we desire more and more to understand God's commandments and serve Him. With our sights on Him, this world is indeed passing away, and our heavenly destination is becoming more the reality.

Suggested Reading: Psalm 39:12; Psalm 119:19; Psalm 119:54; Hebrews 11:13; James 1:27; 1 Peter 1:17; 1 Peter 2:11

Journaling Considerations: Are there some "ways of the world" that you are trying not to assimilate?

_____

_____

_____

_____

_____

Why do you think Peter calls us strangers and pilgrims?

_____

_____

_____

_____

_____

Prayer: *Dear Father God, have mercy on me. Thank you for your grace that sustains me on this journey. I pray that You might count me in your household of faith. Thank you for Your Son Jesus Christ and the Holy Spirit.*

Today's Sweet Tea Moment: May I always pass the time of this pilgrimage honoring God.

Prayer Focus: Missionaries serving God in foreign lands.

Coals of Fire

Jealousy is cruel as the grave:
the coals thereof are coals of fire,

which hath a most vehement flame.

Song of Solomon 8:6b KJV

Jealousy is a fierce emotion which cannot be allowed to take root in a person's heart. We must be diligent to root out all jealousy like we'd pluck weeds from a flower garden. Parents must be wise to discern when normal sibling rivalry has become a product of jealousy, and courageous to correct that situation. I have children, and I teach children. I see this divisive emotion operating all the time. It's an age-old problem, as we can see in the Scriptures.

Proverbs 27:4 says: *Wrath is cruel, and anger is outrageous; but who is able to stand before envy?* Joseph was almost destroyed because of it. He was despised by his brothers, through no fault of his own, because his brothers perceived that their father loved him the most. They hated him, and couldn't even talk peaceably to him. They conspired against him behind his back, and would have murdered him had his brother, Reuben, not intervened.

The Prodigal Son's elder brother was also jealous, even though he was as loved as his brother. When he realized his father was throwing a party because his wayward younger sibling had returned home, he was angry and self-righteous. He wouldn't even go into the house. His father was wise in going out to him, speaking to him in love, entreating him to come in, and explaining his feelings. (Scripture doesn't tell us how the elder brother responded, or how the relationship went on from there.)

In my experience, jealousy, if allowed to take root in one's heart, can distort one's perception of reality, destroy relationships, and cause great personal sorrow. Holding on to jealousy is like holding *coals of fire* in your soul.

Suggested Reading: Genesis 37:3-11; Proverbs 27:4; Luke 15:25-32

Journaling Considerations: Why do you think Solomon chose the image of coals of fire?

Search your heart right now. Is there anyone you are jealous of?

Prayer: *Dear Father God, have mercy on my soul and root out all jealousy from my heart. Heal the hurts in my heart, and those I may have caused, due to the sin of jealousy. Thank you for your love.*

Today's Sweet Tea Moment: The rivalry between Cain and Abel was caused by jealousy.

Prayer Focus: Those who have allowed jealousy to take root in their hearts.

Be Content with What You Have

∽∾∽

*Be careful to guard yourselves against every kind of
greed, because a person's life doesn't consist of the
amount of possessions he has.*

Luke 12:15 ISV

Materialism is "a preoccupation with or stress on material
rather than intellectual or spiritual things," according to Webster's
Dictionary. From my research I learned that materialism has
been a spiritual concern for centuries, even before Ralph Waldo
Emerson spoke out against materialism 200 years ago. Much
of the way we think *is* shaped by the culture in which we find
ourselves.

Who can dispute that our society has become awash in
materialism? We are practically programmed to want all the
newest technology and gadgets, the most comfortable and stylish
homes, cars, clothes, and the most exotic, luxurious vacations.
You name it. We work to afford the highest standard of living
we can possibly attain for ourselves and our families, but when
is enough, enough?

Jesus' parable of the rich man is a parable for our times. This man had so many possessions that he built bigger barns to hold them all—just like we buy bigger homes and put the extra in storage. Self-satisfied, he said to himself: *Soul, you have many goods laid up for many years; take your ease; eat, drink, and be merry.* The parable continues: *But God said to him, "Fool! This night your soul will be required of you; then whose will those things be which you have provided?"* (Luke 12:19-20 NKJV) God calls the man a *fool.* This is a warning to us not to lose sight of the condition of our souls.

Some people, eager for money, have wandered from the faith and pierced themselves with many griefs (1 Timothy 6:10 NIV). How do we guard ourselves and resist the temptation to become preoccupied with things? Paul wrote to the Christians in Rome, *Do not be conformed to this world, but continually be transformed by the renewing of your minds so that you may be able to determine what God's will is—what is proper, pleasing, and perfect* (Romans 12:2).

Suggested Reading: Luke 12:15-20; Romans 12:2; 1 Timothy 6:10; Hebrews 13:5

Journaling Considerations: Do you think that being immersed in materialism prevents us from being available to God?

_____

_____

_____

_____

_____

Are you conformed to this world more so than transformed by God's will or vice versa?

_____

_____

_____

_____

_____

Prayer: *Dear Father God, renew my mind so that I may understand Your will and purpose for my work and my possessions. Help me to lay up treasures in heaven and to concern myself with my soul's estate.*

Today's Sweet Tea Moment: Put God above all else.

Prayer Focus: Benevolence and generosity.

In God's Economy

*The earth is the LORD's, and the fulness thereof;
the world, and they that dwell therein.*

Psalm 24:1 KJV

I've done my share of complaining along with everyone else about this economy. Gas prices, food prices, unemployment—there's definitely reason for concern, but let's get this economic situation in perspective. Whether the stock market is up, or the stock market is down, whether the economy is booming, or unemployment abounds, God, the Creator of the universe, owns everything—all the silver, all the gold, the cattle upon every hill, and even *they that dwell therein.* However little or much we might have, it's all God's. We have what we have only by God's grace. Even our lives are in His hands.

I try to be a good manager of what God provides for me, taking care of my household and, when I am able, helping others who have needs. Other than that, why should I stress? In the media and all around us, people are agonizing over the economy. Some despondent, who have lost their jobs or their fortunes, have committed suicide. I have worried about my own job, as teachers in our county have been laid off through no fault of their own. I've wasted many hours worrying about how I'll ever be financially secure. The Lord has reminded me through his Word to take heed, lest my soul become bankrupt as I worry about the things of this world.

Be on guard, so that your hearts will not be weighted down with dissipation and drunkenness and the worries of this life, or that day will take you by surprise (Luke 21:34 ISV).

God is good. No matter what situation we find ourselves in, no matter how rich or how poor, God loves his children. If we can keep that in mind, and concentrate on our soul's economy, our hearts will enjoy peace, and God will provide all we need in *His* economy.

Suggested Reading: Psalm 24:1; Psalm 50:10; Haggai 2:8; Matthew 6:25-34; Philippians 4:6-7

Journaling Considerations: Do you believe our Creator owns everything?

_____

_____

_____

_____

_____

Do you believe you can trust Him for your needs?

_____

_____

_____

_____

_____

Prayer: *Dear Heavenly Father, whether I am rich or poor, I love you. Whether I prosper or experience lack, I will praise you. Thank you for who you are, and thank you for redeeming my soul. I will trust you all the days of my life.*

Today's Sweet Tea Moment: No man is poor who has received the gift of salvation.

Prayer Focus: Those who live in poverty and those who are lost in sin.

Loaves and Fishes

❦

Then he took the five loaves and the two fishes, and
looking up to heaven, he blessed them, and brake, and
gave to the disciples to set before the multitude.

Luke 9:16 KJV

Five barley loaves and two fish. By most standards, a modest
lunch, yet when Jesus took that food and blessed it, enough was
provided to satisfy the multitude with plenty left over. To me,
this is more than a story about one of Jesus' miracles. It's about
the power of Christ to accomplish God's will even when all He
had to work with was a little boy's lunch.

How could such a meager amount of food satisfy the hungry
crowd? The disciples had seen Jesus performing miracles. They
had walked with Jesus, yet at that moment of basic need—
5000 hungry men plus women and children—they questioned
Jesus. Indeed, the twelve were unanimous in saying, "Send the
multitude away." But Jesus never sends away those in need. One
would think that after having seen all they'd seen, the twelve
would have said, "Jesus, what's for lunch?" Yet they did not. Jesus

did not admonish them. Instead, he demonstrated his divinity by taking the little that was made available to Him, blessing it, and providing for all.

Like that small boy's loaves and fishes, my talents and offerings are meager, yet when they're given over into Jesus' hands to bless and to do with as He wills, miracles happen. Jesus' blessings ensure that needs will be met. All I have to do is approach Him in faith, with a willing heart and open hands. I may not see the results, but they are guaranteed.

My time, my talents, my life—when given to Jesus to bless and use in His service—can satisfy a multitude of hungry souls.

Suggested Reading: John 6:1-15; Luke 9:12-17; Romans 12

Journaling Considerations: Jesus demonstrated who He was by the miracle of feeding the multitude. What had the disciples advised him to do?

_____

_____

_____

_____

_____

What are you willing to give of yourself or of your possessions for His service?

_____

_____

_____

_____

_____

Prayer: *I present myself to you, O Lord, as a living sacrifice. Use me and all I have for your service. Place in me the desire to surrender all, so that Your Kingdom will come, and Your Will shall be done on earth as it is in Heaven.*

Today's Sweet Tea Moment: No gift is too small, no service too humble, when it's given in the name of the Lord Jesus, for His service.

Prayer Focus: Those hungry for *the Bread of Life*.

Let Us Not Be Weary

*And let us not be weary in well doing: for in due season
we shall reap, if we faint not.*

Galatians 6:9 KJV

A close childhood friend came for a visit recently. We've known each other for over forty years, but have seen each other rarely over the last twenty-five. As we shared memories and stories about our families and jobs, decades of personal history lived anew with brilliant fresh meaning.

Childhood dreams might not have been realized, yet life has been rich. Our reunion was particularly refreshing due to this unexpected perk: I could see that perseverance and patience had paid off. Our labors had not been in vain.

We all get weary. Sometimes we are physically exhausted; sometimes we are mentally exhausted, and rather frustrated with the way our lives are going. Maybe the daily routine has become a drudgery which never seems to lighten up, getting harder with each passing day. In a career where we once felt inspired and dedicated to doing good, maybe now we are feeling used up.

I was battling such feelings when my friend came to visit, but as we talked about raising our children, our struggles, and our accomplishments, the precious fruits of our labors came into focus.

Even when we are connected to meaningful relationships and endeavors, many circumstances and outcomes are not what we want them to be, and our patience is tested. In retrospect, it's easier to see that, in spite of life's struggles and pains, we can have confidence in God's promises.

A farmer labors and hopes for an abundant harvest in a season. In a matter of months, he gathers the fruits of his labors. Believers labor and hope for an abundant harvest as well. Fortunately, we see some fruit in this lifetime. Others we will see in eternity. God has promised in due season *we shall reap*, if we do not faint (give up). As we live each day, doing those things that we know we need to do, our confidence can be in the integrity of His word.

Our labors are not in vain.

Suggested Reading: 1 Corinthians 15:58; Galatians 6:9; Hebrews 10:36; Hebrews 12:1; James 1:4; James 5:7

Journaling Considerations: Have you battled feelings of burnout?

_____

_____

_____

_____

_____

Meditate on God's promise in Galatians. Do you have confidence in the integrity of God's word?

_____

_____

_____

_____

_____

Prayer: *Dear Father God, thank you for times of refreshing. Help us to see that your promises are true. Help us not be weary in well doing. Help us run with patience the race that You have set before us, knowing that victory shall be ours.*

Today's Sweet Tea Moment: Don't give up; your labor is not in vain.

Prayer Focus: Encouragement for the laborers in God's harvest.

Hope: An Anchor for the Soul

⋴∽o∽⋼

Why are you downcast, O my soul?
Why so disturbed within me?

Put your hope in God, for I will yet praise him,
my Savior and my God.

Psalm 42:5-6 NIV

The Psalmist's question is certainly sobering. Why *should* we be cast down if our hope is in God? Hope is a vital characteristic of our relationship with Him. In Hebrews, we read that it is a sure and steadfast anchor of the soul. This is a powerful image of holding fast and stabilizing the soul, keeping the believer grounded in the person of Jesus Christ. Hope anchors the believer to God, who is the bedrock of our lives.

We are saved by hope, and we must keep it alive and strong. Life has a way of tossing our boats to and fro. We need that anchor of hope to hold us secure and grounded. God's Word provides enlightenment, edification, and comfort, which increases our hope. The life of Jesus Christ, his death, and resurrection is our "blessed hope" as well, since He is the firstborn, and the forerunner for those of us who believe. Certainly Christ's resurrection is reason enough to rejoice. Prayer strengthens our relationship with God and the Lord Jesus Christ. Scripture tells us to be ready to give a reason for the hope that is within us. Fellowship with other believers and the testimonies of these saints enlivens the hope that lives in our heart.

Our hope does not disappoint. It is named with and strengthened by faith and love. As we place our hope in God, we can rest secure in His promises.

Suggested Reading: Psalm 39:7; Psalm 42:5; Romans 8:24; Romans 15:4; Colossians 1:27; Hebrews 6:19-20; 1 Peter 1:3

Journaling Considerations: Read the suggested Scriptures.

I've listed things that help keep your hope alive and strong. Which of these is the most beneficial for you personally? Why?

Prayer: *Dear Father God, thank you for your mercy and your saving grace. My soul is anchored by my hope, built on You and your righteousness. I praise You, Holy God. Thank you for the blessed hope we have in Jesus Christ.*

Today's Sweet Tea Moment: Those who believe in God are never without hope.

Prayer Focus: Unbelievers tossed to and fro without an anchor for their souls.

He Was a Man of Sorrows Acquainted with Grief

Wait on the LORD; be of good courage,
and He shall strengthen your heart;

wait, I say, on the LORD!

Psalm 27:14 NKJV

Life is difficult. In this fallen world, it can be brutal at times. Times of hardship, grief, and suffering come to us all, threatening to overwhelm our bodies, hearts, and minds. Who doesn't have a friend or relative sick or dying of some disease right now? Who doesn't have a friend or relative going through some kind of hardship? Who has not suffered?

It's pointless and impossible to innumerate all of the painful situations we have experienced or might experience in our lifetime. In light of horrific tragedies, the sin and suffering in this world can break our hearts. Grief can tear at the whole person so fiercely at times that all seems lost in an abyss of despair. How can we endure such times? Truly, it is only by God's mercy and grace. It is the same mercy and grace that sustained Jesus when he lived on this earth, sustained Him in the Garden of Gethsemane as he suffered in his soul, and sustained Him on the cross as He suffered beyond our finite comprehension.

When hard times come, cry out to God. He will hear your cries. Wait on Him. He will strengthen you. Expect to see the goodness of the Lord. Joy comes in the morning. Let it be a consolation to remember Christ's sufferings. Join your suffering to His as a sacrifice for the sins of the world. He was a man of sorrows, acquainted with grief, but He won the victory over sin and death by the power of His resurrection.

Suggested Reading: Psalm 27:11-14; Psalm 30; Isaiah 53:3; Philippians 3:8-14; 1 Peter 5:10

Journaling Considerations: If you are experiencing grief and suffering right now, pray for God to sustain you as He did Jesus in the Garden. Write your prayer.

_____

_____

_____

_____

_____

What gives you strength to keep going through times of pain and suffering?

_____

_____

_____

_____

_____

Prayer: *Dear merciful Father God, I cry out to you. Hear my cry. When I am sick in my soul, my body, or my mind, help me. Strengthen me. I believe in your promises. I will remember Jesus' sacrifice for me. Thank you for your divine mercy and grace. I praise you that you have provided for me the gift of eternal life and joy without end.*

Today's Sweet Tea Moment: Jesus was a man well acquainted with sorrow and grief.

Prayer Focus: Those who are suffering.

The Golden Rule

∽∘∾

Therefore, whatever you want men
to do to you, do also to them,

for this is the Law and the Prophets.

Matthew 7:12 NKJV

I used to be a middle school language arts teacher. My students were a disparate group of preteens and teenagers undergoing the dramatic physical, mental, and social changes that mark the transition from childhood to young adulthood. How did I engage twenty-five to thirty eighth graders in a pertinent discussion to lay the groundwork for the dynamics in the classroom?

For our initial meeting, all eyes were on me. As you can imagine, I needed them to buy into my rules and procedures. I had to make my words personal and relevant to these children with varied life experiences. My words had to resonate with each and every one of them.

First, I presented little scenarios to help them recall their thoughts and feelings in certain situations. As they thought about which kinds of situations, behaviors, and environments made them comfortable or uncomfortable, we discussed how we could each make others more comfortable. At this point, I had their attention. That's when I presented the cardinal rule for all relationships. I proposed that they treat their classmates the way they, themselves, wanted to be treated. This revelation got nods of approval from some, as if it were their idea. From the knowing smiles on other faces, I saw that they recognized this as the "Golden Rule" Christ gave to all mankind.

Jesus spoke these words to the multitudes in his Sermon on the Mount. He wants us to live this way. Practicing the Golden Rule is practicing brotherly love, which works no ill against another. All relationships would be enhanced if people *lived* Christ's command.

Suggested Reading: Matthew 7:12; John 13:35; Romans 13:10; Galatians 5:14; 1 John 4:12

Journaling Considerations: Is it possible to practice brotherly love without loving your neighbor?

_____

_____

_____

_____

_____

Can you think of a time you've applied it to difficult relationships and encounters?

_____

_____

_____

_____

_____

Prayer: _Dear Heavenly Father, help me to live by Christ's words. May all men know that I am your child by my behavior toward others._

Today's Sweet Tea Moment: Christ's commands are the "gold standard."

Prayer Focus: For understanding to apply the Golden Rule to difficult relationships and encounters.

Train the Children

Train up a child in the way he should go: and when he is old, he will not depart from it.

Proverbs 22:6 KJV

My grandson went through potty training at the age of two. He was so proud of himself that he invited an audience. It was amazing how such a little milestone could bring such a sense of accomplishment.

Take it from me, mothers often dread potty training. It can be an intimidating feat for a mother—the first of many. Inevitably, we set our resolve and buy the "big boy" underpants (sporting Thomas the Train, or super heroes, no less). We train our children how to go to the toilet. We train our children how to use a spoon, brush their teeth, say "please" and "thank you." We train them how to behave with siblings, outside the home, at Grandma's house, the grocery store, and church. *Train a child in the way he should go: and when he is old, he will not depart from it.* This is a Scripture full of promise. The essential word is *train*. These accomplishments may seem effortless, but they take purposeful resolve.

The parent is a child's first caregiver and guide. If a child doesn't learn to trust, obey, and respect his parents' leadership and authority, how can we expect him to trust, obey, and respect a teacher, a boss, or God?

God has directed us to teach our children His commandments. *Impress them on your children. Talk about them when you sit at home and when you walk along the road, when you lie down, and when you get up* (Deuteronomy 6:7 NIV). We are to tell our children about His faithfulness.

Not only has God instructed parents to teach their children about Him, He has also instructed parents to discipline their children. I would be remiss if I failed to mention this point. We are to correct our children while there is time. Proverbs 29:15 tells us that a child left to go his own way will bring a mother to shame. Children are intended to be a delight and reward; however, an unruly or foolish child causes much grief and shame to his parents. If we love our children, we must teach them, train them, and discipline them.

Suggested Reading: Genesis 18:19; Deuteronomy 6:6-7; Proverbs 10:1; Proverbs 22:6; Proverbs 29:15-17; Isaiah 38:19; Ephesians 6:4

Journaling Considerations: What does the word *train* mean to you in the context of this story?

_____

_____

_____

_____

_____

As a parent/grandparent, what has been your experience of parenting with "purposeful resolve"?

_____

_____

_____

_____

_____

Prayer: *Dear Lord God, thank you for my children, who are my blessings and reward. Help me to parent them well, teach them of You, and guide them to Your throne of grace.*

Today's Sweet Tea Moment: The Lord disciplines his children because He loves them.

Prayer Focus: The family.

The Lord God Made Us All

❦

With God as my witness, as well as the Messiah Jesus and the chosen angels,

I solemnly call on you to carry out these instructions without prejudice,

doing nothing on the basis of partiality.

1 Timothy 5:21 ISV

When my youngest child was four years old, I was delighted to take him to school with me every day. It was our good fortune that he attended the pre-K program at the school where I worked. All the other students in my child's class, as well as his two teachers, were black. Actually, the population of the school was 99 percent black. We had never discussed race, nor did we discuss it then, but I wondered what he might think about being the only white child in his class.

Robbie quickly made himself at home. Every morning we waited at the front of the school for his new best friend to arrive. Then the two little boys would walk slowly together down the long hallway to their classroom. We adults watched admiringly as the sweet little buddies walked side by side, hand in hand.

One day, at the end of the first month of school, Robbie said to me, "Mommy, all the kids in my class have black eyes."

I hugged him close. "Yes," I said, "they all have black eyes, and their skin is brown." That was the end of the conversation. There was nothing more to say. My heart overflowed with love for my child. To him, the dark eyes were the only remarkable characteristic of each classmate. He never said anything else about racial differences the entire year, as it was insignificant to him. Children don't care about people's race, any more than God does.

As Job so rightly asked: *Did not one fashion us in the womb?* Acts 17:26 tells us: *From one man he made every nation of men, that they should inhabit the whole earth.*

When the Lord spoke to Samuel, who was about to identify the shepherd boy David as King, He said: *For the LORD sees not as man sees; for man looks on the outward appearance, but the LORD looks on the heart* (1 Samuel 16:7b). And so God has called us to do the same. *I, the LORD, search the heart, I test the mind, Even to give to each man according to his ways, According to the results of his deeds* (Jeremiah 17:10 NAS).

Scripture Reading: 1 Samuel 16:7; Job 34:19; Job 31:15; Proverbs 22:2; Jeremiah 17:10; Acts 10:34; Acts 17:26

Journaling Considerations: How does 1 Timothy 5:21 speak to you?

_____

_____

_____

_____

_____

What do you think of Job's question: _Did not one fashion us in the womb?_

_____

_____

_____

_____

_____

Prayer: _Dear Heavenly Father, You created us all. You are no respecter of persons, but look on the heart rather than outward appearances. Create in me a pure heart so that I might see as You see, and love as You love._

Today's Sweet Tea Moment: The inner man of the heart is all that matters.

Prayer Focus: For eyes to see as innocently as little children see.

Be Angry and Sin Not

In your anger do not sin: Do not let the sun go down
while you are still angry,

and do not give the devil a foothold.

Ephesians 4:26-27 NIV

Anger is a universal human emotion which takes on many forms, from quiet sullenness and resentment to outbursts of blinding rage. This Scripture from James is priceless wisdom to anyone who will put it into practice: *In your anger do not sin: Do not let the sun go down while you are still angry.*

I thought of this verse, of all things, at my son Jonathan's wedding reception. He and his bride received a gift from a young couple with the heartfelt message: "Remember to always kiss goodnight." My son and his wife smiled at one another. "Ah, how sweet," they said. In a nanosecond, my mind raced through the years. I know that without God's grace, that directive is pretty hard to follow.

Everyone gets angry sometimes at his spouse. Who can kiss goodnight when he's mad? Who can rest peacefully under those conditions? The verse says, *In your anger do not sin.* To me that means, resolve it, get over it, put it away. If necessary, agree to disagree. Harboring anger gives a place in your soul to the devil. Don't allow him that place. James' word to Christians is: *Everyone should be quick to listen, slow to speak and slow to become angry* (James 1:19 NIV). That is the crux of the matter.

This is good advice for newlyweds and everyone else at home, at work, in the world—don't let the sun go down while you're angry. Let's make it a matter of utmost importance to take control of this emotion rather than letting it take control of us. Don't allow anger to wreak havoc on your mind, body, spirit, and relationships.

Suggested Reading: Psalm 37:8; Proverbs 14:17; Proverbs 22:24-25; Proverbs 29:22; Ephesians 4:26-27; Titus 1:7; James 1:19-20

Journaling Considerations: What physical, mental, or spiritual consequences result when you get angry?

_____

_____

_____

_____

_____

Can any good thing come of unresolved anger?

_____

_____

_____

_____

_____

Prayer: _Dear Father God, thank you for your mercy and grace. I submit my emotions to you, Oh Lord. Help me not to sin against you, for you are righteous and holy._

Today's Sweet Tea Moment: Nothing good comes from unresolved anger.

Prayer Focus: Those with emotional and physical problems caused by harboring anger.

Ask the King of Kings and Lord of Lords

∽ი∾

*When men tell you to consult mediums and spiritists,
who whisper and mutter, should not a people inquire of
their God? Why consult the dead on behalf of the living?*

Isaiah 8:19 NIV

The message was entitled, *Questions Answered* from
"Supernatural Readings," the second message in my email inbox
that day from psychic readers offering their forecasts and advice.
I hit delete without opening such messages, but I have not
always known that God gives us strong warnings in Scripture
regarding psychics. *Do not turn to mediums or seek out spiritists,
for you will be defiled by them. I am the LORD your God* (Leviticus
19:31 NIV).

Like many of my generation, when the Parker Brother's
game, the Ouija Board, was introduced, I received one as a
gift for Christmas. I remember playing it with my friends and
giggling at the possibility of a spooky thrill. Little did I know
then that according to God's word, dabbling in the occult is not

simply fun, it is an abomination unto the Lord.

The occult is all around. Billboards advertise palm readers. Magazines and newspapers regularly print horoscopes. We hear of the rich and famous who consult the advice of astrologers and soothsayers, from present day renowned Hollywood consultants, to Nostradamus in the middle ages. Spiritualists have always been with us. But none of them can save a soul.

Paul lists witchcraft as one of the evil works of the flesh, and he warned that, *those who live like this will not inherit the kingdom of God* (Galatians 5:21 NIV).

Saint John counts sorcerers among those who, *will be in the fiery lake of burning sulfur* (Revelation 21:8a NIV).

The Lord God is a holy God. Trust in His infinite wisdom, His mercy, and loving kindness. When it comes to those things that are hidden, God shields us from them for a reason. He has the answers for today and for the future. Inquire of your God.

Suggested Reading: Leviticus 19:31; Leviticus 20:6-7; Deuteronomy 18:9-12; Isaiah 8:19; Isaiah 47:13-14; Galatians 5:20; Revelation 21:8

Journaling Considerations: If you have dabbled in the occult, you might find the suggested Scripture readings helpful. After reading them, write any new understanding you have gained.

_____

_____

_____

_____

_____

Write your thoughts about this Scripture: *You believe that there is one God. You do well. Even the demons believe—and tremble!* (James 2:19 NKJV)

_____

_____

_____

_____

_____

Prayer: *Dear Holy Father God, forgive me for ever dabbling in any form of the occult, knowingly or unwittingly. Cleanse me, I pray, from all unrighteousness. You are my God. It is You alone I seek. I will look to you for all my needs and trust You for whatever the future holds. All glory is due to you, O God.*

Today's Sweet Tea Moment: The demons know there is only one God and they tremble.

Prayer Focus: Those ensnared by the occult.

His Angels Guard You

⥈⥈⥈

For He shall give His angels charge over you,
to keep you in all your ways.

Psalm 91:11 NKJV

My daughter went to India for five weeks, where she lived with native families while she did soil and water studies. I was excited for her, but also a little apprehensive. Mothers are like that. When my son was stationed in Iraq, I frequently read Psalm 91, filling in my son's name to pray for God's protection. A mother's hands can reach only so far, but God can reach around the world. What comfort it gives me to know God gives His angels charge over us.

For those of us who believe, the existence of angels is a wonderful reality of God's creation. We meet them in Scripture from Genesis to Revelation. Most people are familiar with angels in the story of Jesus' birth. The angel Gabriel appears to Mary to make clear God's plan, and to announce the birth of the Savior. We see many angels in Scripture who appear in dreams to deliver God's messages. We see them going before God's people, fighting their battles, protecting them, leading the way, ever ready to perform God's commands.

Praise the LORD, you his angels, you mighty ones who do his bidding, who obey his word (Psalm 103:20 NIV). God has created all that He needs to serve His purposes. Angels are at His beck and call.

Satan mocked Jesus, quoting a portion from Psalm 91: *If you are the Son of God, he said, throw yourself down. For it is written: "He will command his angels concerning you, and they will lift you up in their hands, so that you will not strike your foot against a stone"* (Matthew 4:6 NIV). Jesus responded with Scripture as well, and when the devil left him, angels came and ministered to Him.

Suggested Reading: Exodus 23:20; Psalm 91:11; Psalm 103:20; Daniel 6:22; Matthew 4:6; Matthew 18:10; Luke 1:19

Journaling Considerations: Are there any particular areas of your life that you would like for God to give His angels charge over?

_____

_____

_____

_____

_____

Prayer: *Dear Heavenly Father God, thank you for giving your angels charge over us. I worship You. Thank you for Your angels who serve your purposes and minister to our needs.*

Today's Sweet Tea Moment: God's angels constantly watch over me.

Prayer Focus: Worship God and give Him glory.

A Pure Fountain

Out of the same mouth come praise and cursing. My brothers, this should not be. Can both fresh water and salt water flow from the same spring? My brothers, can a fig tree bear olives, or a grapevine bear figs? Neither can a salt spring produce fresh water.

James 3:10-12 NIV

Near my home, an artesian spring flows with cool, clear water. People stop by the roadside to fill their jugs from the spring. The water is reliably pure and palatable, arising always from the same source. If that were not the case, no one would bother to stop for the water.

James compares our mouths to a spring. He asks this question: *Can both fresh water and salt water flow from the same spring?* Saint Matthew says that our speech reveals the contents of our hearts: *For out of the abundance of the heart the mouth speaks* (Matthew 12:34 NKJV). Therefore, words flow from the source, which is the heart.

It's interesting that we sometimes state, "I said what was on my mind." More appropriately, we should say, "I said what was in my heart." We know a person's character is revealed by what he says. Duplicity indicates that one is inauthentic, insincere, and lacking in integrity. James says: *My brothers, this should not be.* He also says in James 4:8 NKJV: *Draw near to God and He will draw near to you. Cleanse your hands, you sinners; and purify your hearts, you double-minded.*

Our hearts are purified as we put our hope and trust in the Lord and walk with Him daily. God will renew our hearts so that we can know Him. He will enable us to fulfill his commandments. *You shall love the LORD your God with all your heart, with all your soul, and with all your strength* (Deuteronomy 6:5 NKJV).

He does not expect anything from us that He does not equip us to do.

Suggested Reading: Proverbs 23:7; Jeremiah 24:7; Matthew 12:34-35; James 3:10-12

Journaling Considerations: Do your words and thoughts reflect a heart devoted to God?

_____

_____

_____

_____

_____

What do you think of James' use of the word *double-minded*? When you hear that word, do any images come to mind?

_____

_____

_____

_____

_____

Prayer: *Dear Lord, purify my heart. Let my words flow from a heart consecrated to you. Let me not be double-minded.*

Today's Sweet Tea Moment: Words come from the heart.

Prayer Focus: Pure drinking water for the entire world, and all the environmental efforts that go into making that a possibility.

See No Evil

*He who walks righteously and speaks what is right,
who rejects gain from extortion and keeps his hand
from accepting bribes, who stops his ears against plots of
murder and shuts his eyes against contemplating evil —
this is the man who will dwell on the heights, whose
refuge will be the mountain fortress.
His bread will be supplied, and water will not fail him.*

Isaiah 33:15-16 NIV

After enjoying dinner with my son and his wife one evening, we gathered to watch some television. We flipped through the channels several times, starting and stopping several programs, because everything we saw was saturated with salacious scenes and sacrilege. We even witnessed foul humor about God the Father and the Son Jesus Christ. God's word tells us to withdraw ourselves from ungodly associations. Then why do we become spectators of such things in the name of entertainment?

Every evil thing under the sun is readily available to us now on television, DVD, or the Internet. Should we watch those things that represent the unfruitful works of darkness? *Have nothing to do with the fruitless deeds of darkness, but rather expose them* (Ephesians 5:11 NIV). What is meant by *unfruitful works*? Unfruitful works bring about nothing good, but rather lead to spiritual death. Paul tells us we should actually *expose them*. In other words, have the courage to voice disapproval. *Turn my eyes from worthless things; preserve my life according to your word* (Psalm 119:37 NIV). Not only are we not to *do* the evil thing ourselves, we are not to even contemplate it with our eyes.

Habakkuk 1:13 speaks of the purity of God's eyes. He cannot behold evil. As believers of the Lord Jesus Christ, we are spiritual temples of the Holy Spirit. We receive the Holy Spirit from the moment of salvation. Our bodies and our spirits belong to God. Are we not defiling that temple when we choose to watch all manner of ungodly things? It's no wonder watching certain scenes on television and movies makes one feel uncomfortable, anxious, and, at worst, unclean. Our soul is suffering the *unfruitful works of darkness.*

I will continue to enjoy visual media for entertainment, but I need to choose wisely.

Suggested Reading: Leviticus 20:7; Isaiah 33:15; Habakkuk 1:13; Matthew 5:28; Ephesians 5:11

Journaling Considerations: Do you make thoughtful choices about what you watch, read, or listen to for entertainment?

_____

_____

_____

_____

_____

Have you ever asked yourself if Jesus would be pleased to sit with you to watch whatever programs you are watching?

_____

_____

_____

_____

_____

Prayer: _Dear Father, You are the only Holy and Righteous One that my soul longs to contemplate. Preserve my life according to Your word. Have mercy on me. Give me strength to reprove evil._

Today's Sweet Tea Moment: Honor God in everything you do.

Prayer Focus: Stricter standards and controls regarding television programming.

My Brother's Keeper

❧

And the Lord said unto Cain,
"Where is Abel thy brother?"

And he said, "I know not: Am I my brother's keeper?"

Genesis 4:9 KJV

My youngest son has five older siblings, all of whom in one way or another take it upon themselves to look out for their brother. From the time he was born until now, their joy and love for him compel them to spend time with him and to contribute to his care. Being older, stronger, and wiser than he, they realize they can assist in his upbringing in countless ways. He reaps the benefits of their attention, guidance, and care.

Jesus called *brethren* all those who did the will of His father. As Christians, we follow His example. Those who are weak and needy among us need our attention and care. Like little brothers, they need stronger and wiser brothers and sisters to spend time with them and give them the love and encouragement they need to grow in faith.

My friend Janet first spoke to me about Jesus Christ and

His love in 1977. She has modeled that love through the years. The priceless gift of her friendship and Christian witness has strengthened me through good times and bad. I have been greatly blessed by my Christian sister.

We all need someone to take our hand and guide our steps at some time along the way *till we all come in the unity of the faith* (Ephesians 4:13a).

Suggested Reading: Matthew 12:48-50; Ephesians 4:12-13

Journaling Considerations: Does a certain person come to mind as a brother or sister in Christ who has helped you grow spiritually, or came alongside you to help you in a time of need? What did their help mean to you?

_____

_____

_____

_____

_____

What could you do for someone who has a special need? A prayer, phone call, or some other practical assistance?

_____

_____

_____

_____

_____

Prayer: *Dear Father, show me my brethren, so that I may help care for them. Thank you for brothers and sisters in Christ who have helped me along my life's journey. Thank you for those who have reached out to help me in times of need.*

Today's Sweet Tea Moment: Jesus gave His life for His friends.

Prayer Focus: Those in need of a brother or sister to care for them.

Words of Authority

࿇

His mother said to the servants,
"Do whatever he tells you."

John 2:5 NIV

My youngest son and I used to enjoy our popcorn and movie nights. One night we watched *Back to Bataan*, a WWII film, starring John Wayne as Colonel Madden, a courageous U.S. Marine. The story takes place in the Philippines after the Japanese invasion. Colonel Madden instructs a Filipino resistance fighter regarding the new man in charge, saying, "Do whatever he tells you to do." His words brought to my remembrance the words of Mary, the Mother of Jesus, at the marriage in Cana of Galilee (see John 2).

Jesus and his disciples attended the wedding. When the host ran out of wine for the guests, Mary said to Jesus, *They have no wine.*

Jesus replied, *Woman, what does your concern have to do with Me? My hour has not yet come.*

Then his mother spoke to the servants: *Do whatever he tells you.*

Mary, who knew better than anyone the divinity of Jesus, demonstrated complete confidence—faith—in his power and authority. Jesus turned the water into wine, the first of the miracles He performed on earth to manifest his glory.

I don't know about you, but there are very few people whose words I would follow without question. Yet we are all under a higher authority. Jesus spoke as one having authority; indeed He was given all authority in heaven and on earth by His Father, God. Mary's words are a call to action: "Do it."

Oh, that I would remember her words to those servants every day of my life, and do without question whatever Jesus tells me to do.

Suggested Reading: Matthew 7:29, Matthew 8:9, Matthew 28:18; John 2:1-11

Journaling Considerations: What do you think of Mary's words: *Do whatever he tells you*?

_____

_____

_____

_____

_____

Do your actions demonstrate confidence in God's words?

_____

_____

_____

_____

_____

Prayer: *Dear Father God, thank you for the Lord Jesus Christ and his life, death, and resurrection. Thank you for his blessed mother, Mary. Help me to take her words to heart, and to do whatever Jesus says without question.*

Today's Sweet Tea Moment: Jesus was a man under God's authority.

Prayer Focus: Our military men and women, and those who have authority over us.

A Good Medicine

∽o∾

A merry heart does good, like medicine,
but a broken spirit dries the bones.

Proverbs 17:22 NKJV

The therapeutic value of joy and laughter cannot be denied. Who doesn't enjoy a good belly laugh? I believe I've even heard a story about a sick man who laughed himself well. Charles Dickens wrote in his cherished classic, *A Christmas Carol*: "It is a fair, even-handed, noble adjustment of things, that while there is infection in disease and sorrow, there is nothing in the world so irresistibly contagious as laughter and good-humor." This astute observation brings a smile to my lips. Noble, indeed. God is good.

Job spoke with faith when he said: *He will yet fill your mouth with laughter and your lips with shouts of joy* (Job 8:21 NIV). He expected to see the goodness and joy of the Lord, even though he was in the midst of suffering and sorrow. God wants us to enjoy the life He's given us. The Scripture says that Jesus came so we might have abundant life, which implies ample joy and laughter.

He wants His joy to be a constant and abiding benefit of our relationship with Him. Joy comes from a heart that is content in Christ Jesus.

The LORD has done great things for us, and we are filled with joy (Psalm 126:3 NIV). We need to share that joy with those with whom our lives touch. Share the joy through kind words of encouragement and hope. Share the joy with a million laughs. A happy heart is "irresistibly contagious." It does good to dispense it freely.

Suggested Reading: Psalm 126:2; Proverbs 12:25; Proverbs 17:22; Luke 6:21; John 10:10

Journaling Considerations: What do you think of Charles Dickens' observation that there is "nothing in the world so irresistibly contagious as laughter"?

_____

_____

_____

_____

_____

Do you think God wants His joy to be a constant and abiding benefit of our relationship with Him?

_____

_____

_____

_____

Prayer: *Dear Lord God, You have done great things for me. Thank you for putting joy in my heart and filling my mouth with laughter. Help me find joy in life, and help me to always share it with others.*

Today's Sweet Tea Moment: Laughter does us good like a medicine, plus there's no need to pay a deductible.

Prayer Focus: Those suffering from depression.

Fearfully and Wonderfully Made

❦

I praise you because I am fearfully and wonderfully made; your works are wonderful,

I know that full well. My frame was not hidden from you when I was made in the secret place.

Psalm 139:14-15a NIV

As a mother, my children have been my greatest blessing and joy on earth. My relationship with them has given life meaning and significance. I know each child was meant to be created on purpose, straight from the heart of God. I am happy that God entrusted these precious gifts to me.

Yet, I say from experience, that it is not always easy or convenient to bring a child into the world, to endure high risk pregnancies, to bear another child into the midst of poverty or devastating personal circumstances. Due to God's mercy, I didn't question His sovereignty as Creator. Sadly, many today grapple with decisions regarding the birth of a child based on "reproduction rights" and "personal choice" because God's law, *Thou shalt not kill*, has been perverted to allow for killing life in the mother's womb.

If God creates a life, who are *we* to end it? *All things were made by him; and without him was not any thing made that was made* (John 1:3 KJV). God said, *I kill, and I make alive* (Deuteronomy 32:39). Therefore, if God creates a life, only *HE* should end it.

The great prophet Isaiah spoke to Jacob in Isaiah 44:2: *Thus says the LORD who made you, and formed you from the womb, who will help you.* Did God form Jacob and not form you and me? The Scripture tells us, *For by him were all things created, that are in heaven, and that are in earth, visible and invisible, whether they be thrones, or dominions, or principalities, or powers: all things were created by him, and for him* (Colossians 1:16 KJV). Who are *we* to interrupt God's handiwork, killing His creation before it can even take its first breath? According to Jeremiah 1:15: *Before I formed you in the belly I knew you; and before you came forth out the womb I sanctified you.*

At Christmas time, the movie classic *It's a Wonderful Life* comes to mind. It's an inspiring, life-affirming story of how one person's life touches so many others and transforms an entire town. Watch it with your children during the next holiday season. Maybe you will enjoy this illustration that every life indeed has a purpose.

Suggested Reading: Exodus 20:13; Deuteronomy 32:39; Job 33:4; Psalm 100:3; Isaiah 44:2; John 1:3; Colossians 1:16

Journaling Considerations: Did God form Jacob and not form me and you?

_____

_____

_____

_____

_____

Prayer: *Dear Father God, my soul knows right well that You created us all and have a purpose for each of us. Thank you for the gift of life and giving me the gift of motherhood.*

Today's Sweet Tea Moment: Each life touches so many, it's impossible to know the impact.

Prayer Focus: Expectant mothers. May they choose life, and experience the joy that only motherhood can bring.

Be His Star

Now after Jesus was born in Bethlehem of Judea in the days of Herod the king, behold, wise men from the East came to Jerusalem, saying, "Where is He who has been born King of the Jews? For we have seen His star in the East and have come to worship Him."

Matthew 2:1-2 NKJV

This little light of mine. As a child, I sang this old gospel song with much exuberance. I remember joyfully singing at Bible school and church: "Hide it under a bushel—NO! I'm gonna let it shine."

The inspiration for this song might have come from Jesus' words in Matthew 5:16: *Let your light so shine before men, that they may see your good works, and glorify your Father which is in heaven.* That is our mission.

The glorious gospel of Jesus Christ is light and life to all who will come to Him. Jesus wants us to point the way to Him by living what we believe. Each holy Christmas season, my thoughts turn to the wise men. How beautiful their words while seeking the Christ Child: *We have seen his star ... and have come to worship him.*

The Star of Bethlehem led the way. Jesus wants us to be His stars, shining for the entire world to see, so that by our living faith, in our everyday moments with Him, we will draw all men to the Savior of the world.

Will you shine for Him today?

Suggested Reading: Psalm 148; Proverbs 4:18; Matthew 2:1-2; Matthew 5:13-16

Journaling Considerations: Are you living your life in such a way that others are drawn to the light of the gospel of Christ?

_____

_____

_____

_____

_____

Do you think that is a reasonable expectation?

_____

_____

_____

_____

_____

Prayer: *Dear Heavenly Father, may my life be a light in the darkness of this world—a testimony and a witness for you. May the love of Christ shine through me each day. May I glorify you, Oh God, and draw others to the King and Savior of the world. In Jesus' name I pray. Amen.*

Today's Sweet Tea Moment: Are my words and my deeds drawing others to the Light of Jesus Christ?

Prayer Focus: Place in me the joy of a child singing praises to her Lord and King.

My Personal Journal

_____

_____

_____

_____

_____

_____

_____

_____

_____

_____

_____

_____

_____

_____

_____

_____

_____

_____

_____

_____

_____

_____

_____

My Personal Journal

_____

_____

_____

_____

_____

_____

_____

_____

_____

_____

_____

_____

_____

_____

_____

_____

_____

_____

_____

_____

_____

_____

As You Continue Your Journey

Thank you for allowing me to come with you for part of your journey. I pray God has used *God, Me, and Sweet Iced Tea* to encourage and strengthen you, and to give you hope. I would like to invite you to join the *God, Me, and Sweet Iced Tea* author page on Facebook, where you can engage with me and other readers about this devotional journey. If you believe this devotional might be beneficial to others, please consider writing a review for it on Amazon.com.

For more inspirational messages and encouragement, please visit my blog at: http://www.writemomentswithgod.blogspot.com. I'd love for you to be a part of the Write Moments with God community. If you'd like to write me a personal note, I'd be thrilled to hear from you. Send your messages to writemoments@gmail.com.

And now I leave you with the words of the Apostle Paul:

The grace of our Lord Jesus Christ be with you.
My love be with you all in Christ Jesus.
Amen.

Source Page – Listed by Content Title

1. What Do Our Hearts Tell? – Edgar Allan Poe, *The Complete Tales and Poems of Edgar Allan Poe* (New York, NY: Random House, 1938) 303-306.

2. Action Speaks Louder Than Words – Mark Twain, quote taken from online source at http://www.brainyquote.com/quotes/quotes/m/marktwain162937.html.

3. How Can We Know the Way? – Robert Frost, *The Road Not Taken*. Quote from poem taken from online source at http://www.poemhunter.com/poem/the-road-not-taken/.

4. He Shall Be Like a Tree – Joyce Kilmer, *Trees*. Quotes from poem taken from online source at http://www.poetryarchive.com/k/trees.html.

5. Today Has Enough Troubles of Its Own – Dale Carnegie, *How to Stop Worrying and Start Living* (New York, NY: *POCKET BOOKS*, 1984) 4.

6. Be Content with What You Have – Definition taken from online source at http://www.merriam-webster.com/dictionary/materialism.

7. Be Content with What You Have – Ralph Waldo Emerson. Information taken from online source at http://www.notablebiographies.com/Du-Fi/Emerson-Ralph-Waldo.html.

8. A Good Medicine – Charles Dickens, *A Christmas Carol* (New York, NY: Bantam Dell, 1986) 55.

9. Be His Star – *This Little Light of Mine*. Information taken from online source at http://www.negrospirituals.com/news-song/this_little_light_of_mine.htm.

10. A Word from the Author – C.S. Lewis. Quote taken from online source at http://www.goodreads.com/work/quotes/2072983-till-we-have-faces.

A Word from the Author

To choose the right words, as C. S. Lewis has said, "... to say the very thing you really mean, the whole of it, nothing more or less or other than what you really mean ..." is my challenge when it comes to writing a testimony. For it would be necessary to write volumes to do justice to what the Lord has done in my life. How can words express the greatness of God's mercy toward me? My relationship with Him defines my life and gives meaning to my existence. I truly believe He is the Life that sustains me. I know He restores my soul daily.

I grew up in a tiny rural community in Georgia in a farming family that barely made ends meet. I remember my childhood as an endless barefoot summer, filled with daffodils, dirt roads, and corn fields. As a family, we went to church on Easter and to occasional revivals, but an elderly couple down the street took me, my brother, and two sisters to church every Sunday. A revival came to Sardis Baptist Church, with morning and evening services, and I walked to church that week before the school bell rang and met Jesus as my Savior. I was eleven. I experienced a joyous new birth, but I remained a babe in Christ.

As a very naïve nineteen-year-old, I married and moved to

California. Within a short time, I was at a desperate point in my life due to serious marital problems. In the midst of the crisis, a Christian friend talked to me about Jesus. After we prayed together, I recommitted my life to the Lord and began a true spiritual journey. That was January 1977. Daily prayer and Bible reading quickly drew me into a close personal relationship with the Lord Jesus Christ. As I spent more time reading the Bible and praying, my faith grew—faith that has given me strength for every moment of every day. My salvation didn't change my circumstances, but it changed my soul and gave me a divine helper and hope.

More painful times were to come. Life is difficult, and certain circumstances make it even more so. I've been divorced for many years, and spent most of my adulthood parenting alone. But through it all, my faith in God has given me the strength I need to weather every storm. My greatest joy has come from being the mother of three sons and three daughters. Our family continues to grow as my children marry and have families of their own. I am blessed.

When my fifth child was in kindergarten, I began teaching full time. I've taught both French and English. In addition to two undergraduate degrees, I have a master's degree in counseling and a specialist degree in education. I'm still waiting to do the thing I always wanted to do when I grew up—write full-time.

To say my life has not been easy is an understatement. I have experienced personal heartache, overwhelming obstacles, and disappointments; yet through them all, joy and victories have enriched my life because God is with me. I believe His mercies, which are new every morning, restore my soul daily, and I've grown closer to God as a result of all I have experienced.

My prayer is that this devotional journey has brought you closer too.

*That which we have seen and heard we declare to you,
that you also may have fellowship with us; and truly
our fellowship is with the Father and with His Son Jesus
Christ. And these things we write to you that your joy
may be full.*

1 John 1:3-4 NKJV